Theodore Payne In His Own Words

CALIFORNIA VOICES

This book continues a series which will bring out writings on history and nature from California's past. The texts are either long out of print or have never before been published. The authors speak to concerns of today and we welcome their return. These are authentic California voices.

Also in this series:

Robert Glass Cleland, *El Molino Viejo*

THEODORE PAYNE IN HIS OWN WORDS

A Voice for California Native Plants

*A Collection of Memoirs in
Three Sections:*

LIFE ON THE MODJESKA RANCH IN THE GAY NINETIES
A New Edition

ADVENTURES AMONG THE SOUTHERN CALIFORNIA PLANTS

BRIEF HISTORY OF A LIFE IN HORTICULTURE

Printed for the Theodore Payne Foundation

2004

MANY
MOONS
PRESS

Book design by Mark Morrall Dodge.

Cover design and art direction by Hortensia Chu. She also created the Many Moons Press logo.

Production by Regina Books and printing by Cushing-Malloy, Inc.

ISBN 0-9700481-5-7

MANY MOONS PRESS

P.O. Box 94505
Pasadena, California 91109

PRINTED IN THE UNITED STATES OF AMERICA

Contents

Acknowledgments 7

Foreword.. 9

Life on the Modjeska Ranch in the Gay Nineties

I   A New Life in a New Country - Rattlesnakes -
Washing Our Own Clothes -
Madame and Her Favorite Roses - Other Guests -
A Moonlight Night.. 13

II   Hank Seymour, Horse Trader - George Rock,
a Character 23

III   Abandoned Silver Mines - Moving Soil -
Dante's Inferno - A Stubborn German Lad................. 28

IV   Snap, the Hunter - A Mountain Lion in the Canyon -
Acorns and Woodpeckers - Wild Flowers and
the Garden.. 35

V   Hunting the Flores' Treasure.............................. 41

VI   Interesting Neighbors....................................... 44

VII   Capistrano and the Bullfight - A Water Shortage -
Riding a Bronco Horse 49

VIII   A Birthday Party - Otis Skinner and Madame
Modjeska's Theatrical Company - Six Tons of Honey -
A Railway Strike - A Visit to the Modjeska Ranch -
The Last Time I Saw Madame Modjeska....................... 56

IX   Brief Sketch of Life of Madame Modjeska. 65

Adventures Among the Southern California Plants

The Hitch Hiker 89

Santa Barbara in 1896 93

Laurel Canyon 96

Lost in the Mountains...................................... 97

A Wild Ride to Overtake a Stage Coach 101

A Day on the Desert Without Water 104

Two Royal Coffins.. 108

The Ostriches Didn't Lay Enough Eggs 112

Following the Coast in 1904 114

A Palm Deal 117
Stalled in a Tunnel... 121
Two Tall Palms.. 123
Gathering Grevillea Seed 125
Homer Lea 128
Seed Collecting at Redondo Beach 131
A Carload of Eucalyptus Trees...................................... 132
The Judge's Spittoon 134
The Ombu Tree.. 137
Navarro de Andrade 139
Gathering Eucalyptus Seed.. 143
Two Little Bugs.. 146
The Train was Late 150
Eucalyptus in Libya... 153
The Ants Go to Work 154
The Other Fellow's Shoe.. 156
Baby Quail Crossing a Stream 158
The Game Keeper's Son 160
A Trip to Santa Cruz Island 162
The Stolen Sycamore Seed 165
The Cuff of the Pants 167
Pressed Flowers 169
Chuparosa 170
The Tree He Planted... 173

BRIEF HISTORY OF A LIFE IN HORTICULTURE
A Life in Horticulture 187
Theodore Payne Chronology 201

PAYNE'S LEGACY TODAY
The Modjeska Ranch Revisited 219
The Theodore Payne Foundation and Nursery 220
INDEX OF PLANTS, PLACES AND PEOPLE 221

Acknowledgments

For fostering the publication of this book, many thanks to Frances Schneider Liau and her fellow members of the Theodore Payne Foundation (TPF) Board of Directors: Jennifer Mok, John Wickham, Melanie Symonds and Susan Shum. Elizabeth Pomeroy compiled and edited these texts from the papers of Theodore Payne.

Thanks also to Ellen K. Lee, Corresponding Secretary of the Helena Modjeska Foundation, and Park Ranger Diane Wollenberg, County of Orange, Department of Harbors, Beaches & Parks. Assistance with the Theodore Payne papers was provided by Bea Beck, Head Librarian, and Irene Holiman, Library Assistant, both at Rancho Santa Ana Botanic Garden, and Margaret Robison, Office Manager for TPF. For encouragement and support, thanks to Susan Gottlieb and Catharine Stebbins.

This book was designed by Mark Morrall Dodge and the production was guided by Richard D. Burns. Once again Hortensia Chu has been a presiding spirit, designing the cover and providing art direction for this book to honor the legacy of Theodore Payne.

Financial support for the publication of this book was provided by the Theodore Payne Foundation and the Helena Modjeska Foundation.

Foreword

by Elizabeth Pomeroy

Which comes first, the idea or the doing? This question is not as simple as it may seem. For Theodore Payne, pioneer in cultivating our California native plants, vision and action constantly reinforced each other.

Born in England in 1872, Payne came to California in 1893, having passed his 21st birthday at the Chicago World's Columbian Exposition that year. After several productive years as gardener at the beautiful Modjeska Ranch in Orange County, he embarked on the seed and nursery career that would be his life's work.

Soon after his arrival here, he admired the rich native flora, then saw with regret that the wild flowers were quickly disappearing. He determined to stir up an interest in these natives and began his lifelong specialty. "I collected seed of a few kinds of wild flowers, grew them and offered the seed for sale," he wrote. "Little or no success attended this first venture, it being generally conceded that it was foolish to waste time on 'wild flowers.'"

Clearly the idea needed to be planted first. Then Southern Californians might embrace their bounty of native plants. His method was demonstration plots—in vacant lots of Hollywood and Pasadena, around South Pasadena's famed Raymond Hotel, anywhere he could find open land. Soon the idea was sprouting. When people saw the spring tapestries, they asked for the seeds.

Payne was later responsible for many native gardens (his own designs or plants from his nursery): Griffith Park, Santa Barbara Botanic Garden, Exposition Park in Los Angeles, Rancho Santa Ana Botanic Garden, the native section of Descanso Gardens—the list is long.

But he never stopped planting ideas too. He wrote articles and leaflets with thoughts like: "How to Make a Native Your Friend," or "Be a good Californian: be loyal to your own state and keep your landscape Californian, by planting the trees, shrubs and flowers native to California." Always, he offered something to think about. Perhaps this interplay of ideas and action was the secret of his success, during his 70 years in the field of horticulture.

≈ ≈ ≈

In this collection of memoirs, Payne reflects on his early adventures in Southern California. We see him evolving from pioneer plantsman to crusader, becoming the central figure in preserving and advocating the native plants. These anecdotes show a youthful and vigorous Payne, exploring the mountains, deserts and shorelines of a rich landscape.

The humor and the sheer fun of these adventures will speak to every gardener and traveler. But the message of these stories is more timely than ever. Aware of our needs for water conservation and the silvery beauty of our native plants, we now listen with new appreciation to the voice of Theodore Payne, pioneer plantsman.

The first section of memoirs, "Life on the Modjeska Ranch in the Gay Nineties," reprints a small classic first published in 1962 and long out of print. The remaining two sections are printed here for the first time. All these texts are in the archives of the Theodore Payne Foundation and printed with their permission.

LIFE ON THE MODJESKA RANCH
IN THE GAY NINETIES

Matilija Poppy - *Romneya Coulteri.*

✧ *Chapter I* ✧

A New Life In A New Country
Rattlesnakes
Washing Our Own Clothes
Madame And Her Favorite Roses
Other Guests
A Moonlight Night

NESTLING AGAINST THE HILLSIDE beneath century old live oak trees in the beautiful Santiago Canyon about 20 miles east of the town of Orange stands a low white bungalow, the former home of Madame Helena Modjeska, the great Polish actress who spent so much of her life on the American stage.

Today the grounds are surrounded by a tight wire fence with a padlock on each gate and a great dane warns you not to try to enter. Unless you are a friend of the present owner or can persuade the caretaker to open the gate, you are not going to be able to view this interesting and historic spot except to get a glimpse of the house through the trees. The place is somewhat overgrown with shrubbery, the lawn has disappeared and there are not as many flowers as in former days. But to me it still holds many pleasant memories and my mind harks back to a summer day in July of 1893 when first I set eyes on this charming spot.

I was a young man then, 21 years of age, just arrived from England and looking for a job. I had received a thorough training in the nursery and seed business, so upon reaching Los Angeles it was only natural that I should look up the different seed stores and nurseries here. In this way I became acquainted with James

H. Denham, a Scotchman who owned a seed business on Main Street just south of 2nd Street. Mr. Denham took quite an interest in me from the start and promised to try and locate some work for me. I got a job picking apricots at $1.50 a day but this only lasted a short time. One nurseryman offered me a job budding fruit trees if I could wait till September. Then one day Mr. Denham said, "How would you like to take a position as gardener on a private estate?" He went on, "Madame Modjeska, the famous actress, wants a man for her place in the Santa Ana Mountains, the pay is $35.00 a month with board and room." I told him I was not a gardener but a nurseryman. The latter's work was to propagate young plants and trees, while the former's was to grow these plants on to maturity and bring them into flower or fruit. But if he thought I could qualify, I would be willing to give it a trial. So I decided to take the job.

Now, working in Denham's seed store was a man named Jones and when he heard that I was going to the Modjeska Ranch he tried his very best to discourage me. He said it was a terrible place, that they had a lot of Mexicans and Indians there and they would just as soon kill you as not. The foreman on the ranch was murdered last year, he said. If you go you had better carry a gun in your hip pocket. This kind of took the wind out of my sails. Mr. Denham had told me what a beautiful place it was with such fine people. I did not know what to think. I was really scared. But please remember, I was only twenty-one, having spent my 21st birthday at the World's Fair in Chicago, on my way to California. I was in a strange country and 6000 miles from home.

I talked the matter over with my friend, West Cove, who had come out from England with me and also John Watts, another Englishman who lived in Hollywood. Then the three of us went down to Harper and Reynolds Hardware Store and selected the first and only revolver I ever owned. I fully expected to be a real westerner and carry it in my hip pocket continually.

On the morning of July 18th, 1893, with some misgivings I took the Santa Fe train for El Toro which was the nearest station to the Modjeska Ranch. Arriving at El Toro depot, I was met by a Polish boy named Johnnie Hare, with a buckboard and team of horses. Then a ten mile drive through rolling land, foothills and mountains brought us to the Modjeska Ranch. The horses' hooves made quite a resounding noise crossing the wooden bridge over the creek, then we swung up the driveway and stopped in front of the house.

Madame Modjeska and her husband, Mr. Bozenta, came out to welcome me. They were very nice, democratic kind of folks. He was a former Polish nobleman and his full name was Count Karol Bozenta Chlapowski, but here he preferred simply to be known as Mr. Bozenta.

After unloading some provisions which he had hauled from the depot, Johnnie Hare helped me with my luggage and showed me to the bunk house which was down by the creek. One of the first things he said was, "Where are your blankets? You know, on ranches in this country all the men furnish their own blankets." This was news to me and of course I did not have any. However, Johnnie was good enough to lend me a blanket and got another one from one of the men. Then the first time he went to town I gave him some money to buy a pair of blankets for me.

It was haying time and the men did not come in for lunch but at the evening meal I met them all. The foreman was a German named John Ruopp, a fine looking man, rather tall with blond hair and beard. Two other Germans, one named Heinke, a middle aged man, the other Edward Ziegler, a lad of seventeen who had left Germany before reaching that age in order to avoid having to serve in the army. This was a common practice among German boys in those days. A Frenchman, George Rock, that does not sound like French but it appears he changed his name after coming to this country as a boy, the same as Johnnie Hare, the Polish lad had changed his. Then there was an American, Sid Williams and a Mexican, Joaquin Serrano. This made up the ranch crew. The cook was an old Mexican, Jesus Soto, and there was also a Mexican woman who worked around the house. Now that I was added to the list, six nationalities were represented round the table, quite a cosmopolitan group, and also quite a peaceful looking lot. And, by the way, we ate all our meals out of doors under a beautiful arbor of grape vines.

Where were the wild Indians Jones had told me about? True, I was a little suspicious of Joaquin at first but I soon found him to be a really fine fellow. His family owned the next ranch and he had come over for a few weeks to help out with the hay. The hay, here, I found, was made out of oat or barley straw. This was entirely new to me. Where I came from hay was always made of grass or clover, but I had many things to learn in this new country.

I soon found I had no use whatever for my revolver except to amuse myself by shooting at ground squirrels in the evenings when taking a walk down the canyon.

The ranch consisted of a little more than 400 acres, devoted mostly to cattle raising. There was some grain land, about 30 acres of olives, a small acreage of oranges and grapes, together with an apiary of about 120 hives of bees.

The house, a low rambling bungalow, was designed for Madame Modjeska by Stanford White, the celebrated New York architect and built some time in the eighties. It is one of California's historic spots and many world famous people, including Ignace

Paderewski were entertained here. In front of the house were spacious lawns, two fountains, a large rose garden and flower and shrubbery borders. Then, a little farther up the canyon, was a good sized vegetable garden, the maintenance of which was also a part of my duties.

I soon found I had plenty to do to take care of all of it. Of course, everything had to be irrigated and this constituted the principal portion of the work in the summertime.

The water supply came from the stream in the canyon. A dam had been constructed in the bed of the creek about a mile and a quarter up the canyon and the water carried from there in wooden flumes to a reservoir on a hill back of the house. From here it was piped to different parts of the grounds.

The Mexican woman who worked in the house had a little boy about ten years old named Domingo. The first Sunday I was there he and I went for a walk up the canyon. I was enchanted with the beauty of the scene; the rugged, rocky peaks on either side, the winding trail crossing and recrossing the creek so many times. That beautiful little stream of clear water poured down over boulders forming miniature water falls fringed on either side with trees. Although the grass had pretty well dried up, here and there a late wild flower, like godetia, was still in bloom. At every turn in the canyon a new vista opened up; it was intriguing. I felt as though I must go on and see what was around the next bend; something seemed to draw me on and on. I had never experienced anything like it before and in my joy and enthusiasm I began to run along the trail. Then, all of a sudden, I saw something lying right across the path. I knew instinctively that it was a rattlesnake. I could not stop so I jumped high enough to be sure and clear it. I called back to Domingo to look out. He said it was a rattlesnake and he would kill it; but before he could find a good big stick the snake had made its escape.

About a week later I killed a small rattlesnake in the garden and during the two and a half years I lived on the ranch I killed a good many more. In fact, when I left there, I had fourteen snake skins, mostly rattlers. In those days it was quite a fad to make ladies' belts of snake skins and I had four made up and sent them home to England.

One of the first things I discovered after coming to work on the ranch, was that we had to wash our own clothes. This was a job for Sunday morning and the procedure was to take a round wash tub, a cake of soap, a board and a brush. Then go down by the creek, build a fire and heat a tub full of water, throw the clothes in the tub, then take them out one at a time, lay them on the board and scrub with the brush, rinse out in the creek and hang up to dry.

Our clothing requirements were very simple and consisted principally of a pair of blue overalls and a shirt. In fact, no one thought of wearing any other kind of clothes. If you were going to visit one of the neighboring ranchers or one of the beekeepers who lived in the different canyons, or perhaps ride over the trail to Silverado Canyon to see the pretty young school teacher, you would simply put on a clean shirt and a clean pair of overalls, then you were all dressed up. No one ever thought of wearing cloth clothes unless he was going to the city.

In the fall, Mr. Ruopp hired an Indian to come and chop a supply of firewood. His name was Antonio and he brought with him a squaw whom the boys called Cachora (lizard). I don't know what her real name was. An old house a short distance away, on the other side of the creek, was provided for them to live in. We soon made a deal with Cachora to do our washing. Antonio would come over and collect the clothes and take them home. After they were washed he would bring them back and collect from each one of us the amount due. It worked out fine and we were all glad to abandon our Sunday laundering by the creek.

One day I went over to the shack where Antonio and Cachora lived and there on the windowsill was a long row of bulbs of the soap plant or amole. I asked Antonio what they were for and he said, "Amole, amole." "Yes," I said, "I know what you call them but what do you do with them? Do you eat them?" "No, no," he said, "Washy, washy." To my great surprise I found that the old squaw washed all our clothes with these roots. You never saw a better job of laundering anywhere, the clothes were spotlessly clean.

In the Santiago Canyon it gets pretty hot in the summertime and I found it a little trying at first. I had to put in long hours to keep up with all the work, nevertheless I enjoyed it. One thing that interested me very much was the large number of swallowtail butterflies which flitted around the garden, also the little hummingbirds. We had swallowtail butterflies in England though they were rather rare, but the hummingbirds were entirely new to me and I never got tired of watching them dart so rapidly from flower to flower.

Madame Modjeska used to come out and walk around the garden every day. She was passionately fond of roses. I remember one of her great favorites was the Papa Gontier. There was a very good assortment of roses on the place. I do not recall all of them but I do remember the following:

Papa Gontier, Catherine Mermet, Madame Caroline Testout, Duchess de Brabant, Perle des Jardins, La France, Marie Van Houtte, Maman Cochet, Paul Neyron, Magna Charta, Ulrich Brunner, Prince Camille de Rohan, General Jacqueminot, Captain

Christy, American Beauty, Reve d'Or of Lamarque, Beauty of Glazenwood, Reine Marie Henrietta, White Banksia.

Many of these old fashioned roses one rarely sees in gardens today. Perhaps the newer roses are finer but to many of us these old favorites will always linger in our memories.

In the afternoons Madame and her friends would generally occupy chairs or hammocks on the lawn under the oak trees and read and chat or do fancy work. Later in the afternoon they would go horseback riding. Madame rode a bay horse she called Orlando.

This was a fascinating place and such lovable people to be associated with. Besides the natural beauty of the scene the whole air seemed charged with gaiety and romance. It was indeed a new experience for me and sometimes I wondered if it were not all just a beautiful dream.

The days were rather warm but the evenings were delightful and I often enjoyed a walk down the canyon, after which I would sit out of doors and listen to the crickets and other night sounds.

Among the house guests was Miss Josephine Tuholsky from San Francisco. She was the lady who taught Madame the English language, making it possible for her to appear on the American stage. Madame thought a great deal of Miss Tuholsky and always called her Jo. I remember, like Madame Modjeska, she was exceedingly fond of roses and greatly admired those in the garden. Before she left I arranged to send her, in the fall, cuttings of some of her favorite varieties.

Other guests who had been entertained this summer were Mr. and Mrs. James Rice who had a beautiful home in Tustin, the Yochs of Santa Ana and the Langenbergers of Anaheim. Mrs. Langenberger was quite a gardener and had many rare plants at her place in Anaheim. In later years I visited her home on several occasions and she also came to my nursery in Los Angeles. Her daughter, Mrs. Bullard, was also interested in horticulture and distinguished herself by being the first person to hybridize the Watsonia, having over fifty named varieties to her credit. Florence Yoch, then a little girl, has since become a famous landscape architect and is responsible for the laying out of many beautiful gardens in Southern California.

In September Madame and her husband left for the theatrical season and we more or less settled down to a winter schedule. Old Jesus Soto, the Mexican cook, left for Los Angeles. Mrs. Ruopp, the foreman's wife, came up from Santa Ana and she and her husband lived in Madame's house. Our dining quarters were transferred from the grape arbor to a room next to the kitchen and Mrs. Ruopp did the cooking.

There was a small one room shack built against the hillside under an oak tree just beyond the grape arbor. This was supposed to be for the gardener. But while Madame was home it was occupied by her maid. Now they had all left, I moved into this shack. The rest of the men continued to occupy the bunk house down by the creek.

I remember one occasion not very long after moving into this room. I had been reading a very interesting book and it was now about eleven o'clock, long past my usual time for retiring. It was a beautiful moonlight night and for some unknown reason I felt an urge to step outside for a moment. The garden and trees looked so wonderful under the soft light of the moon. Then something caught my eye that startled me. Sitting at the table under the oak trees, on the lawn, was what appeared to be a man with his hands on the table and his head buried in his hands as though weeping, or in a state of despair. What on earth could a man be doing here at this time of night and who could he be? There was no one in Madame's house as the Ruopps had gone to Santa Ana and the men were all in the bunk house down by the creek.

Maybe it was a crazy man who had wandered up into these mountains? My first impulse was to go to bed and forget it but then I knew I wouldn't sleep but would keep wondering about that man out there at the table, so I decided to investigate. If he appeared dangerous I could run pretty fast.

I walked boldly toward the table and when I came a little closer I saw what it was. Our big black retriever dog, "Oso," was sitting on the seat with his front paws on the table and his head down on his paws. I said, "Oso, what in the world are you trying to do? You nearly scared the life out of me."

✧ *Chapter II* ✧

Hank Seymour - Horse Trader
George Rock - A Character

George Rock, the Frenchman, was a strange character. He was a rather small man but very strong and a splendid worker though he did not appear to derive much benefit from his labors. He would work hard for a few months, save all his money, then go to town and blow it in. On reaching Santa Ana he would make straight for a saloon and set up drinks for everybody. The word spread like wildfire that "Old George" was in town and the thirsty ones were on hand in no time. After the first few rounds he did not know whether he received any change or not, and usually he did not. Five dollar gold pieces, one after another, went over the counter and by nightfall George's money was gone.

I remember one time George had been working steady for three months. He got thirty dollars a month and board. In addition to this he received twelve dollars a month pension from the government because he had served in the civil war. So he had well over a hundred dollars saved up and wanted to go to town. Johnnie Hare was going to Santa Ana with the wagon and team so he took George along. On the evening of the third day after this Ed Ziegler and I were reading in one of the back rooms of the shack used as the bunk house when we heard someone knocking on the front door and talking in a very loud voice. Ed went out to see what it was and came back in a minute all excited. He said, "There's a man out there wit whiskers like de Lord!" Ed was the seventeen year old German lad and knew very little English. He

23

had evidently seen pictures of English Lords and wanted to say, "With whiskers like a Lord."

I went out with him and there was the strangest individual I had ever seen. A tall, gaunt fellow of middle age with mutton chop whiskers, talking in a very loud voice and using the most profane language and drunk as could be. He wanted to know where George was. I told him George had gone to town with Johnnie and they had not yet returned. But he kept on, "Where's George, by God, I know he's here. I am Hank Seymour. Where's George? Where's Johnnie?" Mr. and Mrs. Ruopp were up at Madame's house, Johnnie had not come back from town and Sid Williams had gone to see old man Harding in the next canyon. So Ed and I were alone; this strange looking individual had appeared on the scene all of a sudden; we did not know where he had come from or how he had gotten here or who he was and we were anxious to get rid of him. I tried to convey this idea to him but he only talked louder and swore more. Ed was all excited and said, "I'll get rid of him." He ran into his room and grabbed a revolver. Here was a near tragedy; an excited German lad with a gun and a crazy drunk. No one knew what might happen. I said, "Ed, for God's sake, put that gun away. That man's drunk. We must handle him some other way." I finally persuaded Ed to put the gun back.

This queer specimen of humanity, whoever he was, kept talking louder and swearing more and still wanted to know where George was. I tried again to explain that George was not here. But he kept on. "By God, I know he's here. Where's his room?" I said, "George sleeps in that little room at the end of this one, back of that curtain, but he's not there." Then Hank got up and strode over to the other end of the room and said, "George, get up and come out of there." To our utter astonishment he dragged

George out by the collar of his coat. "George," he said, "come out here and tell these fellows what a good time we had."

It then developed that George and Hank had been on a grand spree together. George had spent all his money; treated everybody, bought a new dress for the bartender's wife and was now thirty dollars in debt. He had to get back to the ranch and Hank had brought him up with his horse and buggy. How they drove in and put the horse in the barn without us hearing them is a mystery. How George got into his room without us knowing it is another mystery. Most likely he crawled through the window. He wanted to sleep and soon went to bed but Hank was just the opposite, he was wide awake. He swore, told stories and sang songs.

A little later Johnnie arrived with the wagon and team. I told him about this strange character and asked him what to do. "Oh," he said, "that's old Hank Seymour, he will be all right tomorrow." So Johnnie found a place for Hank to sleep and we finally got him to retire.

The Ruopps knew Hank quite well and invited him to spend a few days on the ranch. When sober, he was quite an interesting fellow. He had been a very good lawyer but drink had got the best of him.

Somehow he found out that I was in the market for a saddle horse and I believe he planned from that moment to sell me one. At any rate, he invited me to go back to town with him and stay at his house; which I did. He had a house, barn and an alfalfa patch in Santa Ana, quite a nice little place.

Mrs. Seymour was a very sweet little woman and quite pretty. Hank thought a lot of her but was very abusive when drunk and she had a hard time. She put up with him as long as she could but finally got a divorce and married another man who made her a good home and treated her well. He must have been a very fine man for I understand, when poor old Hank got sick, he let her go and nurse him till he passed away.

The Seymours were very hospitable folks and made me feel quite at home. They told me whenever I came to town to come and stay at their house as they would always have a room for me. This was very nice and I afterwards took advantage of their hospitality on several occasions.

Hank had a little bay mare he called Dolly. He said she would make a good saddle animal for me. He was to take me back to the ranch on Sunday afternoon so he hitched Dolly up to the buggy and we started out. He evidently expected to make the trade for he took a saddle along so I could ride the mare. He also had an extra horse tied to the back of the buggy so if he made the deal he could get back home. He talked about the merits of this little bay mare a good deal of the way and when we were in the canyon, about eight miles from the ranch, he took Dolly out of the buggy and put the saddle on her and I rode her around for awhile. He had used her for driving but she was pretty good under the saddle and had a nice easy lope. I guess Hank was a good trader and I was somewhat of a tenderfoot; at any rate he talked me into the deal and I gave him fifty-five dollars and became the new owner of Dolly. Hank hitched up the spare horse to the buggy and returned to Santa Ana while I proceeded on to the Modjeska Ranch, arriving there after dark.

Both Johnnie and Mr. Ruopp thought that Hank had put over a pretty slick deal and had gotten the best of me. I think, myself, forty dollars was about the real value of the animal. However, I didn't hold anything against Hank even if he did get a little the best of me on a horse trade; the hospitality he and his wife afterwards showed me more than made up for this.

Dolly turned out to be quite a good little saddle animal. I had lots of fun riding around the country and made many trips to Santa Ana. I afterwards sold her to Gus Baum who had a bee ranch in one of the side canyons. He thought a lot of her and she had an easy life, spending most of her time in his pasture with an occasional trip to town for supplies.

✧ *Chapter III* ✧

ABANDONED SILVER MINES
MOVING SOIL
DANTE'S INFERNO
A STUBBORN GERMAN LAD

AS THE WEATHER was now getting cooler it was not necessary to do so much irrigating, but there was plenty of other work to do. During the last winter the creek had risen with the heavy rains and had sliced a piece of land from the garden, perhaps ten or twelve feet wide. George had spent two or three months building a rock wall to keep the creek in its place. It was now my job to fill in back of this wall with soil. Mr. Ruopp let me have Ed to help me, also a team of mules and a dump wagon. This dump wagon was a crude affair, the bed of which was made up of a number of 2 x 4 timbers. These were shaved up at each end into a sort of handle. When it came time to unload one man would go to each end and loosen up these timbers one at a time, letting the earth fall through. We got the soil from a hillside back of the vegetable garden. First we would take a plow and the mules and plow down some soil from the hillside, then load it into the dump wagon with shovels. Then plow down another lot. Some days we would haul as many as eight loads. How many loads we moved altogether I do not remember, but I am sure it was well over a hundred. Every time we plowed down a new batch of soil we would disturb some scorpions and centipedes and occasionally a tarantula. At first we made a collection of these creatures, putting them into glass jars. However, we soon got tired of this so just destroyed them. Ed could speak only a very little English and I did not know a word of German, so it was up to me to teach him. I found him a good pupil and he picked up the language very quickly. Soon I had him singing little songs in English. Hauling soil was hard work but we did not mind it. These were happy days. We had lots of fun and were always ready for our meals. In the evenings we used to gather round the table after supper and play poker or casino.

About this time a new man came to work on the ranch. His name was August Goss, a young fellow about twenty-four years of age, a German by birth, who, I believe, had come to this country when a boy and had worked on farms in Missouri. He had very light hair, in fact so light it was almost white. Old Jesus, when he came back to resume his job of cooking, nicknamed this fellow Cavasablanca, meaning white head, but most of us called him Gus. He was a very good worker and used to handling teams.

Being from Missouri, many things were new to him out here and he always had to be shown. One day he came up into the garden and seeing an olive tree loaded with the ripe fruit, he said, "What are they?" "Oh," I said, "those are olives." "Gee," he said, "can I have some?" I told him, "Just help yourself." So he began picking olives and putting them in his mouth. Then he started to cuss in both English and German. I thought he would never get through. He was terribly sore; but I said, "I didn't tell you they were good to eat. You asked me if you could have some and I told you to help yourself, you can't blame me." But he never got over it.

There were a number of abandoned silver mines in the canyon above the ranch and one Sunday Gus and I went exploring these mines. We had two burros on the ranch, Jack and Jenny. Jack was somewhat bronco and would buck every time you'd get on his back for perhaps a distance of fifty yards, after that he was all right. I put a saddle on him and rode him while Gus rode Jenny bareback. We took our lunch with us and made a day of it. Burros are the most obstinate creatures you ever saw; they go when they want to and just as fast or slow as they want, also. Jack was a real good saddle animal after he got over his little performance and would travel along pretty well. But Jenny was terrible! She would poke along and stop and you would wonder if she was ever going to move again! So we did not make very good time. The trail follows the creek and crosses and re-crosses it many times. We came to one place where there was a deep pool. I expected Jack to follow the trail and go around over the rocks, but to my surprise he took one leap and we landed on the other side. Then along came Jenny and she thought she'd do the same thing. She took a jump but did not quite make it and landed right in the middle of the pool and there she stood. Gus was quite tall; I wish I had a picture of him now astride that burro in the middle of that pool. He pulled up his long legs to keep his feet out of the water. I can almost hear him now.

"Jenny, get up. Get out of here! Jenny get up, get out of here." Then his language became more choice but no amount of cussing or coaxing or pounding could move that burro. There she stood in the middle of the pool. After awhile, when she got good and ready she quietly climbed out and up onto the trail.

The mines are tunnels running into the mountain sides. We lit candles and explored all these tunnels; in some cases the timbers had rotted and some of the earth had caved in. I have often thought since that it was not a very wise thing to go into these old abandoned tunnels, but you do things when you are young that you would not think of doing in later years.

After going to the end of all these tunnels we returned to the ranch feeling that we had been on quite an adventure.

My friend, West Cove, who with his wife and little daughter had come out from England with me, and later had settled in Hollywood, came and spent a few days with me on the ranch. He was quite a good amateur photographer and took a number of pictures, including a very good one of Madame Modjeska's house, also some interesting spots in the canyon. He enjoyed his visit very much and, of course, it was quite a new experience for him. I remember he was rather shocked at the manners, or rather, lack of manners of some of the ranch hands. At the dinner table it was a case of everybody for himself or you'd get left; "Pass the beans!" "Pass the spuds!" etc., but they were really a good hearted lot of fellows.

We were now having beautiful moonlight nights and one evening after supper I suggested to my friend, West Cove, that we take a walk down the canyon. After walking about a mile, I turned left on the trail leading up a little side canyon. I said, "In a little while you are going to have the surprise of your life. I am going to show you 'Dante's Inferno.'" The trail came to an abrupt end at the edge of a precipice, and spread out before us the whole terrain appeared to have sunk, leaving thousands of jagged rocks of fantastic shapes and forms standing erect. The formation is of reddish sandstone and on a moonlight night creates a most weird effect. You come on to it so suddenly it just takes your breath away.

My friend said, "I don't wonder you call it 'Dante's Inferno'!" I said, "That's my name for it, the people around here call it the 'sinks.'"

Johnnie was going to El Toro next day with the buckboard so my friend went along and took the train back to Los Angeles, after a few very pleasant days spent on the Modjeska Ranch.

Soon after this Emil Goepper, a carpenter from Santa Ana, came to stay on the ranch for awhile to build a new dining room onto Madame's house. He was quite an interesting fellow, well informed and, besides being a carpenter, had had some experience in the nursery business, so we had something in common.

While he was on the ranch, we went on several trips exploring some of the different canyons. On one occasion Emil Goepper, Ed, Gus and I went up the Harding Canyon. We stopped and chatted with old man Harding for awhile then continued on up the trail. A few miles beyond the Harding place we met an old man coming down the trail mumbling to himself. When he saw us he implored us not to go on. He said, "The devil is up there." The poor old man was just about exhausted. We told him to keep on down the trail and he would come to the Harding place and Mr. Harding would give him food. On our way back we found the old man had arrived all right; Harding had fed him and he was now resting comfortably. How he happened to be up there in the canyon I never heard. It is possible he had come clear over from Temescal on the other side of the mountains. Harding said he would ask him to stay a day or so until he recuperated.

On another occasion, we went up our canyon then followed the left fork for quite a distance. It was a beautiful canyon but not much of a trail. We noticed a small peak which looked attractive and we debated whether we should climb to the top of it. It was getting late in the afternoon so we decided against it, that is, all except Ed. He said, "I go." I said, "Ed, it's too late in the day to start climbing peaks. You had better stay with us." All I got for an answer was, "I go. I go." I couldn't do a thing with him. Off he went, that stubborn German lad and we did not see anything more of him for an hour. We reached the main canyon and it was now getting dusk. I said to Emil, "I am getting real worried about Ed. He should have caught up with us by now. He's such a stubborn, bull-headed fellow. You know he's only seventeen and hasn't much sense. He may have met with an accident." A little later we heard the brush crackling and breaking and here emerged Ed with his clothes all torn and dirty. It seems he had climbed to the top of the peak, then realized that it was nearly dark and started to descend too rapidly. He had come to a small cliff and before he could stop had gone right over it. Luckily he landed in a lot of brush or would probably have been killed.

On another occasion we went to a place they call the "Rock Island" which covers perhaps an acre of ground or more. It has sheer straight walls except in just one place where it is connected with the rest of the terrain by a narrow ridge, so narrow that you can straddle it with one leg on each side, like sitting in a saddle. By using your hands you can hitch yourself across, but when you get there, there is a very difficult climb up onto the island. It is said that only one man had ever made it. Ed, of course, had to try it. When he got about half way across he looked down at the chasm to the right and the one on the left, then the climb ahead of him and he gave up. He said, "I can't make it." I said, "Then come on back." He said, "I can't get back." By this time I was a little out of patience and I said, "I told you not to try it, now you can just stay there." He found it harder to return but finally made it.

One day, I think it must have been the next summer, Ed caught a live rattlesnake. He put it in a box and placed a glass over the top. He kept it in his room under the bed. We had heard that snakes went a long time without food, but after about a month we thought the snake must be in need of a meal, so one Sunday we caught a live mouse and put it in the box with the snake. We stood by breathlessly waiting to see the snake devour the mouse, but nothing happened. The mouse sat in one corner and the rattlesnake in another. We thought perhaps the snake did not like having spectators at mealtime so we went away. After about two hours we returned, fully expecting to find the mouse gone, but there it was, still sitting in the corner of the box. The snake did not seem to be paying much attention to the mouse and the mouse did not seem to be particularly frightened. However, we felt we had done our duty in offering the snake a meal and if it wanted to go on a hunger strike, that was all right with us. So we let the mouse out of the box and it ran off and probably told the rest of the mice about its strange experience and they most likely called it a liar.

Incidentally, I put my finger on the glass covering the box and the snake struck at it. My arm flew back involuntarily and I tried it again, but could not keep my finger on the glass. Ed said he could do it, he was always very positive about everything. Full of confidence, he put his finger on the glass. The snake struck and his hand flew back. He couldn't do it any more than I could. By this time the rest of the gang had gathered around the box, including two cow hands from another ranch. They were all positive they could do it and were ready to bet on it. They all tried but the moment the snake would strike at the glass their hands would involuntarily fly back.

Ed kept the snake for about three months, then let it out one day and killed it. He skinned it and gave the meat to old Jesus, the Mexican cook, who melted it down for rattlesnake oil.

We used to kill a number of rattlesnakes on the ranch every summer, and old Jesus would collect the oil and sell it to a drug store in Sonoratown, Los Angeles. Incidentally, the old devil used to adulterate it with other fats. If the druggist followed the same procedure, it would be difficult to estimate how much real rattlesnake oil the customer would obtain for his money.

Chapter IV

SNAP, THE HUNTER
A MOUNTAIN LION IN THE CANYON
ACORNS AND WOODPECKERS
WILD FLOWERS AND THE GARDEN

THERE WERE THREE DOGS on the ranch. Oso, a great big black retriever; Buckhorn, an old spotted dog, and Snap, a black and tan hunting dog. Snap was a great hunter, he seemed to be almost human. If I were inclined to believe in reincarnation then I should say that Snap had been some great hunter in a previous existence.

After supper Snap would come and stand in front of you and bark, as much as to say, "Come on, let's go hunting." Then, not getting any response to this invitation he would grab your wrist with his teeth and try to pull you along. Still not getting any encouragement he would try someone else. After going the rounds without any results he would start out by himself. Soon you'd hear him barking somewhere down the canyon. Someone would remark, "Snap's on the trail of something." A little later he would give a few short, quick barks, followed by a few more short, quick barks. Then one of the boys would say, "Snap's got something tree'd, let's go."

The poker game was stopped, we'd grab the guns and a lantern and go out and get whatever it might be. Generally it was a fox, sometimes a bob cat and occasionally a raccoon. One time we got a tame cat by mistake. We had several cats on the ranch, one of them an old gray cat with short ears and a head shaped something like a wild cat. One night Snap got this cat tree'd a short distance down the canyon and Johnnie shot it, thinking of course that it was a bob cat, but when it dropped from the tree it turned out to be this poor old gray cat. I felt sorry, for it was a nice old cat, and Snap, I think, felt ashamed of himself when he saw it lying dead on the ground.

One night Snap fooled all of us. He had something tree'd on a hill back of the house. We took a lantern and started to climb though it was awfully steep and no trail. One of the group remarked, "How can he have anything tree'd up here? There are no trees on this hillside, only brush." That was true, there were no trees on that slope. Nevertheless, Snap kept barking and the sound came from one spot, he was not traveling. So we kept on climbing and climbing, finally we reached the spot and there was Snap and all he had was a skunk up in a Sumac bush.

Not all our hunting was done at night. One Sunday afternoon when returning from Silverado Canyon I heard Snap barking in a side canyon. I rode up there and found he had a great big bob cat in an oak tree. It was about a mile and a half from the ranch buildings and I got there as quickly as possible. I told Johnnie and he took his rifle and I grabbed a shot gun. When we reached the spot Johnnie shot at the cat but missed, then I opened up with a shot gun. I hit the cat but did not kill him and he jumped to the ground and started to put up a fight with the dogs but old Oso grabbed him and that was the end. Oso was not a hunting dog but he and Buckhorn always went along with us, they seemed to like to be there at the kill. Buckhorn was too old to put up a fight, but Oso was a powerful animal and when he once got hold of a victim it was good-bye.

This wild cat was a big fellow. I skinned him and sent the skin to a taxidermist in Los Angeles and had it cured and the head stuffed.

I remember one day, Johnnie came running through the vegetable garden. "Come along, get a gun!" he cried. "We've got a mountain lion tree'd up the canyon." It seems that he and Carl Ziegler, Ed's brother who was now also employed on the ranch, had gone up the canyon to clean out the flumes which carry the water to the reservoir, when Snap had routed out a mountain lion and got him up a tree. Carl stayed on the spot with Snap while Johnnie ran home to get a gun. It was about a mile and we saddled two horses and lost no time in getting there. Johnnie told me where the tree was and I knew the spot exactly but before we got there we saw Carl standing in the trail. Johnnie said, "Where's the lion, Carl, this is not where I left you." "He's up in this oak tree," Carl replied. "After you left the lion jumped down and Snap and I chased him down the canyon and he went up this tree." Johnnie was all excited and very nervous but got the lion with the second shot from his rifle. He had the specimen stuffed and mounted and it stood for a long time in Madame Modjeska's house.

This was the first mountain lion killed around there for several years, though old man Harding in the next canyon had killed nine during the time he had lived there.

Early in 1894 Mrs. Ruopp returned to Santa Ana and Jesus Soto came back to do the cooking. The cookhouse and dining room was moved to one large room in the shack down by the creek. This building was just a wooden shack built with up and down boarding and a redwood shingle roof. The other half of the building was used as a bunk house.

In one room I noticed the cheesecloth ceiling had sagged down in one spot and it looked as though some heavy object had been placed there. I called the attention of some of the other fellows to it but not one of them seemed to have any explanation. What it was or how it got there no one knew. As the weeks went by it grew heavier. One day my curiosity got the best of me and I took a long handled broom and gave the object a poke. It turned out to be an accumulation of acorns and they began to roll in all directions. There must have been at least half a bushel of them.

In the fall of the year the woodpeckers collect acorns and store them in the trunks of trees, in this section, usually sycamores. They drill a hole in the trunk of the tree just large enough and deep enough to hold the acorn. Sometimes you see whole patches of them set in very close together. Evidently the woodpeckers thought the redwood shingle roof was an easy place to drill holes but they did not figure that when they pushed the acorn into the hole that it would go through. When it did they kept putting in another and another and this accounted for the accumulation of acorns above the cheesecloth ceiling of our bunk house.

About five miles down the canyon grew the giant white bush poppy (*Romneya coulteri*) generally known as Matilija Poppy. Mr. Bozenta asked me to collect some seed of this plant and grow it in the garden. I gathered the seed, prepared a bed and sowed the seed but nothing came up. I did not know then, as I do now, that had I burned some straw or dried grass over the ground, I would have succeeded in germinating the seed. In later years I used to collect this seed in Silverado Canyon for exporting to Europe. Also found plentifully down the canyon was a yellow Bush Penstemon (*Penstemon antirrhinoides*). This, too, I collected in later years.

There were a number of wild flowers that attracted my attention, among them a very pretty blue larkspur. Also the Violet Beard Tongue (*Penstemon heterophyllus australis*), and a lilac colored Mariposa Lily. In some of the shady spots the Meadow Rue grew six feet high.

One Sunday three or four of us went to a place called Elephant's Peak, so named because it was shaped like an elephant. In the canyon bottom at the foot of this peak the maidenhair fern was so tall it came up above our knees, great bushes of it. I have never seen anything like it anywhere else.

In the vegetable garden, when Madame was at home, I tried to have as large a variety of vegetables available as possible. After she left I concentrated on the most staple varieties for the ranch help.

Among the flowers the roses predominated and occupied quite a large area. There was also a considerable space devoted to ornamental shrubs including a number of double pink oleanders, Bird of Paradise shrub and Turk's Cap (*Malvaviscus mollis*). The hummingbirds were very fond of these last two. A number of plants of Japanese Wineberry grew luxuriantly and bore most delicious fruit. I have never seen this plant anywhere else. A long border was devoted to Cannas, there was also a border of *Gazania splendens* and one of the silvery leafed Lamb's Tongue (*Stachys lanatum*). There was a wooden fence at one end of the garden covered with the Blue Dawnflower (*Ipomoea leari*), a perennial morning glory which was a glorious sight all summer. On each side of the walk from the driveway up to the house there was a Canary Island Date Palm. The one on the left hand side had died and Mr. Bozenta told me to replace it. I ordered one about five feet high from James H. Denham in Los Angeles and in due time the plant arrived. I started to dig the hole for it and had not gone more than ten inches when my shovel struck a rock. I thought it was just a small one and tried to pry it out with the shovel but could not move it. I then began to dig the earth away. I worked all morning and by noon I had unearthed a boulder more than three feet in diameter. I said, "No wonder that poor palm died. It was planted on top of a rock."

After lunch Johnnie brought up a team and we put a chain around the rock and pulled it over by the creek. We then hauled in a little extra soil and I planted the palm. There were quite a number of young plants of the California Fan Palm (*Washingtonia filifera*) which have since grown into large specimens. There was a single plant of the Abyssinian Banana and one jacaranda, both of which were frozen back each winter. We had some cold weather each season and on one occasion the ground was frozen hard so that I could not get a spade into it for two days, even in the middle of the day.

◇ *Chapter V* ◇

HUNTING THE FLORES' TREASURE

JESUS SOTO was quite a character. He was born in Mexico and educated for the Church, but he did not like that kind of a calling and so had worked at all kinds of jobs. He had a great gift for acting. Sometimes he would put on a one man play that would keep us all laughing. He would walk around the supper table, all the while making up a story bringing each one of us into it. He generally called me "Cuatrojos," meaning "four eyes" because I wore glasses, though sometimes he would simply refer to me as "El jardinero," the gardener. Old Jesus was very good to me. Nearly every afternoon about 3:30 or 4:00 o'clock he would call me down to the cookhouse to have a cup of coffee and a piece of cake or pie or whatever he happened to have on hand. I can almost hear him now, he would come to the lower end of the garden and call out, "Hey, Cuatrojos, quieres café?"

Opposite the Modjeska home is a rocky projection known as "Flores' Peak"; so-called after a noted outlaw of that name. The story of the bandit, as I recall hearing it, goes something like this.

Flores and his band of outlaws were camped on the floor of the canyon; everything seemed quiet and peaceful; then one of the band looked up and saw Andreas Pico and a posse coming down the slope over which the El Toro Road now passes. The outlaw raised the alarm and the bandits hurriedly mounted their horses and started up the canyon. About half a mile above the spot where they camped the canyon divides, the right fork going up by the Modjeska place, the left fork to what is known as the

Harding Canyon. Instead of following one of the canyons, the outlaws took to the hogback, or ridge, dividing the two canyons, but after going a short distance they discovered that this fell off into rocky cliffs. Thus they were caught in a sort of trap. To go on was next to impossible, and to turn back would be to fall into the arms of the posse. The story goes that Flores buried a treasure on this spot and people have dug holes all over the top of this peak looking for it. In one place there is a steep slide down part of the cliff, and it is said that the outlaws forced some of their horses down this and they were killed; most of the bandits got down somehow and hid away. Two were captured and were taken a few miles down the canyon and strung up on a tree.

While I was on the Modjeska Ranch, George Rock, one of our men, left and went to work for J. E. Pleasants on a ranch about two and a half miles down the canyon. One day while working there George unearthed two skulls. Mr. Pleasants said they were the skulls of the two members of the Flores' band and showed George the tree nearby from which they were hung. J. E. Pleasants was the oldest settler in the canyon and had formerly owned the property where the Modjeska residence was built. Eventually, Flores was taken prisoner and tried and executed in Los Angeles.

Well, Jesus told me a story about the Flores' treasure. He said he was acquainted with an old Mexican woman in Los Angeles who knew Flores and talked with him before he was executed. He confided to her the place where he buried his treasure. He said, "You go up Santiago Canyon and up on the mountainside to the left of the left fork is a green meadow. You can see it for miles before you come to where the canyon divides. In this meadow is a spring and by the spring is a flat rock. Under this rock the treasure is buried."

The story did not make much of an impression on me, but Ed Ziegler became quite excited and immediately wanted to go and hunt for it, so one Sunday morning he and I started out on a treasure hunting trip.

We went up the Harding Canyon for quite a distance and then started climbing up the mountainside. After climbing a long time we came to a small mesa covered with low brush, mostly chamise and manzanita. We found bear tracks but did not see any bears. We crossed this mesa but could not find anything that looked like a green meadow. After this we came into an area covered with buck brush. It was so dense that in a few minutes we did not know in which direction we were going. Sometimes we had to crawl on our hands and knees and it seemed as though we would never get out. The worst of it was we did not know whether we were getting deeper into the thicket or not, and for all we knew, we might be going around in circles. I said, "Whatever we do, we must stay together."

Well, after a long time, it possibly seemed longer than it really was, we got out again and we were truly thankful. We were tired and dirty and hungry. Our enthusiasm for hunting buried treasure was at a low ebb. We both said, "Let's go home." So we returned to the ranch and it was long past the lunch hour when we got there, but good old Jesus came to our rescue and how we did eat.

We did not find the Flores' treasure, or the flat rock or the spring, or even the meadow. But there in the Santiago Canyon you can see in the distance, away up on the mountainside, to the left, an open green patch just as the bandit described it to the Mexican woman. How to get there? That is another question.

✧ *Chapter VI* ✧

INTERESTING NEIGHBORS

THERE WERE A NUMBER of interesting people living in these mountains. In the left branch of the Santiago Canyon, about a mile away, Isaac Harding had a bee ranch. Everybody called him "Old Man Harding." He had lived there a long time and had had many adventures. He came from a good family back east, was a well educated man and kept up on current events as much as anyone could living in these mountains. Like other bee keepers he just managed to eke out an existence from his bees. A good year and he would be flush, then a dry season or two and he was broke. He lived there all by himself. His wife got tired of living in the mountains and preferred to live in Santa Ana.

Though Isaac Harding lived by himself he liked to have visitors and quite frequently had someone staying there for a week or so. I remember Sid Williams who was one of the men on the Modjeska Ranch when I first went there, was out of a job and old man Harding said, "Come and stay with me, Sid, till you get something to do." One summer evening I walked over to the Harding place and Sid was sitting on the steps of the cabin. "Where's Old man Harding?" I said. "Oh, he's gone to town." Sid replied. "But I expect him back tonight." It was a beautiful moonlight evening and we sat on the steps and talked while Harding's two dogs lay curled up on the ground. All of a sudden both dogs jumped up. "The old man's coming," said Sid. "How do you know?" I asked. "Why, the dogs heard him," he said, and sure enough both dogs trotted off down the canyon to meet their master. It was quite awhile before we could hear the wheels of the buggy grinding on the rocks where the road crosses the creek. But dogs have a much keener sense of hearing than we humans have. At least, we so-called civilized ones.

Old man Harding had had some very interesting experiences. Quite frequently he would locate a nest of wild bees and when a sufficient quantity of honey had accumulated he would rob the nest. On one occasion the bees were in a hollow trunk of a tree. It was really a large branch which had grown out sideways and had been broken off. He had been watching this nest for some time and concluded it was just about time to take out the honey, when one morning he went out there and found someone else had had the same idea. There were bear tracks all around and it was very evident that Mr. Bear had got there first, also that he was not quite tall enough to reach the hollow trunk so he rolled a rock up and stood on it to get at the honey.

On another occasion he found a swarm of bees in a cave. He crawled in on his hands and knees and felt something cold under his hand. To his horror he discovered that he had his hand on a rattlesnake's head. Fortunately, he had presence of mind enough not to raise his hand. He pressed down with all his weight and crushed the snake's head against the rock floor of the cave. When he came out of the cave he shook like a leaf and was a nervous wreck for several days.

In many ways the old man had plenty of courage. He wasn't a bit afraid to go out at night by himself and trail a mountain lion or a bear, but if a horse he was driving would balk he would become panic stricken.

Everybody knows what a common weed the horehound is in California. When or how it came here I do not know, possibly the Padres brought it. At any rate, Isaac Harding was responsible for helping spread it, at least in the Santa Ana Mountains. He read in a Bee Journal that the horehound was a very good honey producing plant and that it would grow under very dry conditions. So he sent for a quantity of the seed. At that time he also kept goats and when the goats were in the corral at night he would dust some of the seed on their backs and then the goats would scatter it over the hills.

In a side canyon about a mile below the Modjeska Ranch lived August Baum, another bee keeper. He was an old bachelor and lived all by himself. He kept a horse and a small wagon and would occasionally make a trip to Santa Ana for supplies. His shack was just big enough for one person to live in and the canyon was not very interesting being devoid of trees. It seemed to be a favorite haunt for tarantulas and almost any summer evening you could see three or four of these strange creatures crawling around. Tarantulas were in demand by the curio stores in those days and Baum used to catch them and deliver them to Santa Ana.

A few miles down the canyon was the ranch of J. E. Pleasants. He was quite a horseman and every year was judge at the County horse show. To many people he was known as Judge Pleasants. Besides raising fine horses he had cattle, bees and some grain land. Mrs. Pleasants was fond of flowers and had quite an attractive garden.

A few miles further on, in Silverado Canyon, lived an old Stanford professor by the name of Benton Julian. He had a cabin perched up on a small flat overlooking the canyon. He kept bees and had a few fine horses. He was a fine looking old gentleman with a gray beard. A very interesting man to talk to and I spent many pleasant evenings at his place. His son, Ed Julian, had a homestead in another canyon and there was also a family by the name of Opp.

Two Englishmen, Tom Hughes and Harry Hughes, lived in Silverado Canyon, both of them were miners and both had large families. There was also a family by the name of Allsbauch living there. The last place up the canyon was the Masons. Mrs. Mason, her son Charlie and daughter Clara. The latter taught at the Silverado School. This school was made up mostly from the Hughes and Allsbauch families.

About three miles over the grade on the road to El Toro was the Serrano Ranch. There was quite a large family of the Serranos, five sons and one daughter, I believe. I remember passing by the ranch one Sunday. I had met all the boys but had never seen the old folks before. I heard one of the boys tell them that I was El Jardinero from the Modjeska Ranch. It was about noon and nothing would do but that I should come in and have a meal with them. So in a few minutes I found myself sitting at a table in the old adobe house with a plate of carne con chile and tortillas and frijoles before me. I never met more hospitable people anywhere in my life. The Señor and Señora did not speak English and I had not acquired much Spanish, so it was difficult to carry on a conversation but the younger members of the family acted as interpreters so we got along pretty well. The old folks did not have very much to say anyhow, but just sat and beamed at me. They really seemed pleased to have me there and I felt that I was an honored guest.

The sons were fine strapping young fellows and great horsemen. They always had plenty of saddle horses on the ranch.

The families mentioned comprised our nearest neighbors. There were several English families in El Toro but that was ten miles away. Occasionally, on a Sunday, I would visit some of them.

A favorite pastime for Sunday afternoon was to run races with our saddle horses. There was a straight piece of road about a mile and a half down the canyon just right for this purpose. Our bunch would meet with some of the Serrano boys and a few others and race our horses. We sometimes made small bets but never lost or gained very much. However, we had a lot of fun.

✧ *Chapter VII* ✧

CAPISTRANO AND THE BULLFIGHT
A WATER SHORTAGE
RIDING A BRONCO HORSE

WE HEARD THERE WAS to be a bull fight at Capistrano on a Sunday afternoon so decided to go. There were four of us in the party, Johnnie, Ed, Gus and myself.

Among the horses on the ranch was a little sorrel mare named Fanny, quite a good driving animal, just a trifle larger than my mare Dolly. Johnnie thought they would make a good team and wanted to try them out. So we hitched up Fanny and Dolly to the buckboard and started for Capistrano. Neither of them had ever been driven double before and when Dolly wanted to go Fanny would balk and when Fanny started Dolly would balk. We had quite a time getting them going but after they once started, they traveled along pretty well. We went by way of Laguna Beach, In those days the road did not go through Laguna Canyon as it does today, but went from El Toro through Aliso Canyon. We arrived at Laguna Beach about noon and had lunch at the hotel, an old wooden building which stood on the same site as the present hotel.

After lunch we proceeded on our way, that is as soon as we could get our team started. We had to go through the same performance as before but finally we got them both going and we were on our way to Capistrano and the bull fight.

It wasn't a real bull fight, they turned a bull loose and played with it with a red flag, then when it charged they stepped quickly out of the way. Not really very exciting but still it called for quite a little skill.

The place was full of men on horseback. There was Marco Forster from the great Forster Ranch, on his big sorrel horse with silver mounted saddle and bridle. Judge Egan, of course, was there. These two were looked upon almost as the rulers of Capistrano in those days. I think there had been plenty of wine on hand for everybody seemed very happy. In the late afternoon, everywhere, you could see Mexicans sitting outside their dwellings playing guitars and singing the sweet Spanish songs. Not a single fight or brawl, everybody seemed to be having a good time. I never saw such a happy contented lot of people anywhere in my life. Now, looking back over the years that have passed since that time, I feel that it was a privilege to have seen and experienced a little of the spirit of California of those earlier days.

We spent a little time at the old Mission which interested me very much, especially as it was the first of the California Missions I had seen.

After going through another performance with our balky team, we started back to the ranch. Driving these two mares together was not a success and we did not try it again.

The winter of 1893 and 1894 was very dry. I do not remember how much rain we had but it seems to me it was less than six inches. The following summer, consequently, found us short of water.

About a quarter of a mile up the canyon was a small spring and it was the general opinion that by tunneling into the hillside a supply of water could be developed. So Mr. Ruopp hired a miner named Joe Ernwright to come and drill this tunnel. Joe worked at it for quite awhile, several months I believe it was. Every night at the supper table he would tell us what kind of a day he had

had and how much progress he had made with the tunnel. Some days he did better than others but always according to his story, the little stream of water had increased. Some days it would be a quarter of an inch, some days more. If the results had only been half as good as he claimed, there would have been plenty of water to supply the whole place. But, alas, when the tunnel had been driven seventy-five feet or more into the hillside, the amount of water was actually the same as when it was started, so the project had to be abandoned.

In a side canyon, above the present dam, was an old water system which had been abandoned when the present dam was built. The pipes were still there but disconnected in several places. Johnnie Hare went to work and repaired this old pipe line and we had water for awhile. But, as the summer season advanced, this supply gave out.

In front of the Modjeska home was a well with two oaken buckets. The ranch provided me with a team, a light wagon and three large barrels and I hauled water from this well to water the roses and shrubs. It was very slow work, drawing the water up a bucket at a time from the well, emptying it into a barrel, then baling it out again and carrying it to each plant, but it was the only way I could keep things alive. The first day I worked at it all morning and started again after lunch. By 2 o'clock the well was empty. The next day I emptied the well before noon and a few days later by 11 o'clock. After about three weeks I could empty this well before breakfast. So I had to find a new source of supply.

A short distance away, where the canyon forks to go up to the Harding place was an old shack and a well. From this well I could draw three barrels of water, then I would have to wait an hour or so for the water to seep in again. I made four trips a day, three barrels to the trip. After a few weeks I threw out one barrel and later on tossed out the second one. Toward the end of the summer all the water I could get was one barrel four times a day. I had to ration the water, giving each rose bush or shrub just enough to keep it alive. I managed to keep most of the plants alive. The lawn, of course, I let die out and re-sowed it the next spring. The rose bushes looked terrible but I cut them back severely in the late fall, then gave them a good top dressing of manure. The next spring they put on a good growth and the roses were better than ever. The folks did not come to the ranch that summer but went to Europe, if I remember right. This was very fortunate, for Madame would have wept to see her roses and everything else almost dead.

In the late fall I took a few days off and went to visit my friends, the Coves, in Hollywood.

I was very anxious to see Madame Modjeska on the stage. She had already played in Los Angeles and was now appearing in *Macbeth* at the opera house on Raymond Avenue in Pasadena. In those days there were no street cars to any of the outside towns and the only way to get to Pasadena was by train and the trains did not run very often. I took the train in the afternoon to Pasadena, engaged a room at a hotel, went to the theater and came back on a train the next day.

Before returning to the ranch I bought a saddle horse from a man named Harnett at Toluca. It was a dark brown, almost black, cow pony named Kitty. She was the easiest riding animal I have ever known. She had been trained to single foot, though on a long trip a slow trot was a better gait. On a lope it was just like sitting in a rocking chair. I rode to Santa Ana the first day, stayed the night there with some friends, then went on to the ranch the next morning. Now for awhile I had two saddle horses, then I sold Dolly to Gus Baum who lived in a canyon back of our olive grove.

Jose Serrano had a big sorrel horse with a white face which was considered to be about the best saddle animal anywhere around, for which he asked the sum of one hundred dollars. Ed Ziegler had saved up quite a little money and wanted to buy a saddle horse, nothing would satisfy him but the best so he bought this big sorrel from Jose.

This horse had been quite a bronco; Jose had a hard time breaking it in and it would still buck a little when you first got in the saddle. Ed had never done much riding and after purchasing the horse he was afraid to ride it, so he asked Johnnie Hare, who was a good horseman, to ride it around a little first. This Johnnie did, the horse would buck for a few minutes, then quiet down, then Ed would get on and everything was all right. Ed and I generally went somewhere on Sunday, that was about the only time we had for riding. So we went through this same performance every Sunday. Johnnie had to ride the horse first and he was getting quite puffed up about it, he bragged that Ed was afraid to ride his own horse and that he, Johnnie, had to ride it for him. One Sunday Ed said, "I hate to ask Johnnie to ride my horse first every time I want to go anywhere." I said, "I have been wondering how long you were going to keep this up, why don't you ride the horse yourself?" Ed said, "I am afraid he would buck me off." "Well," I said, "Let me ride your horse and you ride mine." "Oh no!" he replied, "I am sure he would throw you off." "That's my look-out," I said, for I was planning to use a little strategy. I knew when two horses are used to going together, if one starts off the other does not want to be left behind and will follow the first one. "Now, Ed," I said, "You get on my horse, and when I tell you to go you start right off and don't wait for me." After I had given the signal I slipped my foot in the stirrup, swung my leg over the saddle and the horse started off after the other one without ever thinking of stopping to buck. My strategy had worked and we never had any trouble after that. Pretty soon the horse forgot all about bucking. I have often thought since that many of these horses that buck when first mounted are probably trained to do so, the rider wants to show off a bit and makes the horse buck, the horse gets to know he is expected to put on a little show and does it out of habit.

I don't know why, but for some reason we got the idea that we should train our horses to get used to the sound of firearms, so we got a quantity of blank cartridges and would fire off our revolvers when on horseback. One day we put on a sort of a show. We came in shouting loudly and firing at each other with these blank cartridges. Some of the boys on the ranch took it quite seriously, they thought it was a real fight. This was before the days of the movies.

Ed and I went on many trips together; Laguna Beach, Trabucco Canyon, Silverado Canyon, Hidden Ranch and other places. I remember on one trip to Santa Ana, after we got down into the valley near Tustin, the fog was so thick we could not see the trees on the side of the road. Never, even in London, had I ever experienced anything like it. We had to trust entirely to the horses to find the way. Ed was ahead of me and I could hear his horse's hooves on the road. We talked to each other, yet I could not see the faintest outline of him or his horse. It was one of the most peculiar sensations I have ever experienced.

Later on Ed left the ranch and put his horse in Gus Baum's pasture. He made me promise to ride the horse once a week to keep him in training. I did this, religiously, for awhile, then I missed one week; two weeks; three weeks; pretty soon it was six weeks. I said to myself, "I really must ride that horse or he will get bronco again." So I went to the pasture, caught the horse and brought him up to the corral. After lunch I had just finished putting the saddle on when along came Alphonso Serrano, we always called him Bob. I said, "Bob, I'll give you a dollar if you'll ride this horse for ten minutes." "That horse!" he said, "Why, I wouldn't get on that horse for twenty-five dollars, he almost killed me once when Jose had him." Then along came Johnnie Hare. "I'll bet you a dollar he throws you, off," he said. "No," I replied, "I don't want to bet." "I'll bet you five to one he throws you off." He came back. "Perhaps he will," I said, "but I am not betting on it." I knew Johnnie was aching to have me ask him to ride the horse but I would not do it. I really thought the horse would buck some for he had been in the pasture six weeks and I was a little bit scared. I examined the saddle to see if I had it cinched up tight enough to hold but not so tight that it might make the horse buck. Then I got on. Nothing happened. He was as quiet as a lamb. I have often kicked myself since that I did not make that five dollars.

I made another trip on horseback to Los Angeles, stopping the first night with some friends in Santa Ana and going on to Hollywood the next day. I returned to the ranch about a week later.

✧ *Chapter VIII* ✧

A BIRTHDAY PARTY
OTIS SKINNER AND MADAME MODJESKA'S
THEATRICAL COMPANY
SIX TONS OF HONEY
A RAILWAY STRIKE
A VISIT TO THE MODJESKA RANCH
THE LAST TIME I SAW MADAME MODJESKA

THE RAINFALL during the winter of 1894 and 1895 was much better than the previous year so our water supply was replenished.

Early in the spring I re-seeded the lawn. The grade was perfect so I simply loosened the surface with a rake and sowed the grass seed. I had no sooner gotten the seed sown when it started to drizzle. This weather lasted for nearly a week and was just made to order. I got a beautiful stand of blue grass, then burr clover began to come up and there was quite a heavy stand of this. It seems that a few years before a quantity of goat manure had been spread on the lawn. This evidently contained burr clover seed and this seed had been lying in the ground waiting for favorable conditions to germinate. This meant a lot of weeding. I had a little Mexican boy to help me and every afternoon we spent several hours weeding the lawn. It took the two of us several weeks to get this completed.

In the spring of 1895, when Madame Modjeska came home, she brought with her a young girl, a member of her theatrical company, Miss Maud Durbin, whose home was in Colorado. She was a very sweet girl; everybody liked her and all the boys on the ranch were devoted to her in no time. The roses were all in bloom and Miss Durbin spent considerable time in the garden, so I naturally saw a good deal of her. She used to come out in the morning and walk along the paths as she practiced reciting some of her parts. The little Mexican boy who helped me weed the lawn just could not understand it. A lady walking alone talking to herself? I noticed him watching her one day with a very puzzled look on his face. Finally he could not stand it any longer. Coming up to me he pointed at Miss Durbin and said in a rather pitying voice, "Señorita loco, muy loco."

This young girl, though of course no one knew it at that time, was later to become Mrs. Otis Skinner and the mother of the now famous Cornelia Otis Skinner.

One day Miss Durbin said to me, "Do you ever catch any moles? I have been told mole skins are very beautiful and I wish I could get one." "Yes," I said, "A mole has a beautiful skin and back in England where they are plentiful I have seen gentlemen's fancy vests made entirely of mole skins. Out here we have lots of gophers and I am trapping them all the time but so far I have not seen any moles."

"Well," she said, "If you do find any, please remember me." I told her I would do my best. I had never wanted a mole before and now I wished one would come along. Then, as if in answer to my prayer, one day while I was irrigating some shrubs I saw something pushing up the ground. "Oh," I said, "Here is just what I have been waiting for, a mole." I picked up a hoe and in another minute had the creature out and killed. I skinned it, cured the skin and gave it to Miss Durbin. She was quite pleased and said she would have a small coin purse made out of it.

One day, while some of us were talking down at the bunk house, Johnnie happened to make the remark that his birthday was on June 18th. "Well," I said, "That's a strange coincidence, my birthday is on June 19th." Then we found we were both the same age: twenty-three years. Johnnie said, "We'll have to celebrate. What will we do?" Someone suggested that we send to Santa Ana for a keg of beer; get some of the boys together and have horse races down the canyon. This was pretty well decided on, then Johnnie happened to mention it to Madame Modjeska and her husband, Mr. Bozenta. They said, "Why not have a barbecue? You can kill a steer, we have plenty of them on the ranch. We can invite the neighbors and some of our friends." So our little party grew into a big party. Johnnie and I went up to the house two or three evenings, practicing dancing with Madame and Miss Durbin.

The day before the celebration some Mexicans arrived on the scene and took charge of the ceremonies. A steer was brought in from the range and slaughtered. A big hole was dug in the ground and a fire made in it. After the fire had burned out, the head of the steer was wrapped in sycamore leaves and placed in the hot ashes and covered up with earth. The next day at noon this was dug up again, the hide peeled off and the meat was ready to serve. The head cooked this way is considered the choicest part of the animal. Of course, there is not very much of it but the flavor is delicious. The rest of the meat was barbecued over an open fire. There were plenty of tortillas and frijoles and wine and beer. People came from all over the countryside; ranchers, beekeepers, laborers, Americans, Mexicans, Indians, everybody goes to a barbecue. I think there must have been nearly eighty people there. We had foot races, sack races, horse races and other sports. In the evening we had a dance on the veranda of the house. There was Madame Modjeska, one of the greatest actresses the world has ever known, by many considered second only to Bernhardt, dancing with Jose Serrano, wearing a big Mexican sombrero. What a picturesque scene. I thought to myself, "What a wonderful country. No where else could this happen. Hospitality and freedom. No social lines or barriers and everyone happy and contented." It was an experience I shall never forget and it all came about because two fellows working on a ranch happened to have their birthdays at the same time.

A little later in the season, Madame Modjeska's whole theatrical company, including Otis Skinner, the leading man, came and stayed over the week end at the ranch. There were quite a lot of them and we had a hard time finding room to accommodate them all.

Otis Skinner was a charming fellow and was much interested in the garden and everything on the ranch. Some of the members of the company had never been out west before and it was quite an experience for them, visiting a ranch in the mountains of California. Some of them went horseback riding, others enjoyed walking up the canyon and admiring the scenery. Some were interested in the apiary and in hearing about the life of the bees, extracting the honey, etc. They asked some rather foolish questions about wild animals, snakes, tarantulas, etc. I believe they all enjoyed their visit to the Modjeska Ranch. Among the group was a sister of Miss Durbin and she stayed about a week longer than the others.

The spring and summer of 1894 was a very poor season for the honey crop on account of the dry winter. There were very few wild flowers and the bees barely made enough honey to keep them alive. The next year, however, owing to the copious winter rains, there was an abundance of bloom on the white and black sage, buckbush, sumac, wild buckwheat and all the other kinds that make up the chaparral, so the bees were very busy collecting honey. When the comb in the hive is filled with honey, the forms holding the comb are taken out, the honey extracted, then the forms are put back in the hive and the bees fill up the comb again with another lot of honey. This process is repeated several times during the season and the last filling is left in the hive for the bees. How many extractions there were during the season I do not remember, but the total output amounted to about one hundred pounds of honey to the hive, or six tons from the 120 hives.

John Ruopp looked after the apiary and did the extracting. Sometimes Johnnie or one of the others would help him. I was not supposed to do any of this work but on two or three occasions I put on a net and gloves and helped Mr. Ruopp just for the experience I would get. This came in handy for a few years later, one Sunday morning, when visiting some friends in Hollywood, there was a swarm of bees on their front porch and they were in a quandary as to what to do. I got a box and "took" the swarm. My friend's house was on the corner of Sunset Boulevard and Cahuenga, so there were a good many people passing there on their way to the San Fernando Valley. I put up a sign, "Bees for Sale," and before the afternoon was over I had sold them.

After the honey season was over, Mr. Ruopp left the ranch to accept a position with the American Beet Sugar Company at Chino.

It was now late summer and Maud Durbin was planning to leave the ranch and spend a few weeks with her folks in Colorado before the theatrical season opened. We were feeling rather sad for we knew we would all miss her on the ranch. Johnnie took her and her baggage to El Toro station. Then, to our surprise, when Johnnie came back Miss Durbin was still with him. A railroad strike was on and there were no trains running. This was the time that President Grover Cleveland called out the militia to put the United States mail through.

On account of the strike, we could not get any fresh meat. Of course, we could kill a steer but that would hardly pay for so few people. Old Jesus had on hand some carne seca (dried meat) which he had cured at the time of the barbecue, but this was not like having good fresh meat. I overheard Madame say how they missed having any meat for the table and I thought perhaps I could do something to help remedy this situation. Often, of a summer evening, I would take a walk down the canyon and shoot rabbits. I rarely got more than one for they were not very plentiful. On this particular evening, however, I was more lucky than usual for I got three nice young cottontails. I took them up the house and Madame and Mr. Bozenta were delighted.

Mr. Bozenta was a charming person, highly educated, well read, very sociable and he loved to talk. We had many interesting conversations. He was also very absent minded. He used to smoke a great many cigarettes and I remember on one occasion we were talking and he asked me if he could roll a cigarette for me. At that time I smoked a little, a habit I later discontinued. Upon my affirmative answer he proceeded to roll a cigarette for me, then calmly put it in his mouth and lit it. I, of course, could not say anything. Then a minute later he found his mistake and said, "Oh, how stupid of me! I am smoking two cigarettes." He then proceeded to roll another one for me. He used a special brand of Turkish tobacco, a large box of which arrived by Wells Fargo Express each season.

If I remember right, it was about two weeks before the trains were running again and Miss Durbin finally left. The next time I saw her was a few years later after she had become Mrs. Otis

Skinner. One day in Los Angeles she and her husband called to see me at Germain's, where I was working, and brought me some tickets for the theatre. A few weeks after Maud Durbin left the ranch, Madame, her husband and maid, Anastasia, all left for the theatrical season.

This had been a lovely summer and the garden was beautiful with lots of roses and other flowers in bloom. Besides Miss Durbin, Madame had had a number of other visitors for a few days at a time including the Rices of Tustin, the Yochs of Santa Ana and the Langenbergers of Anaheim. Something was going on all the time and there was joy and gaiety in the air, but after they all left, it was terribly dull and lonesome.

My duties, besides taking care of the grounds around the house and the vegetable garden, included the pruning of the olive trees, of which there were thirty acres about a mile down the canyon. If I remember right it took me something over two weeks to complete this work. I used to take my lunch and stay all day. Often I would not see a soul all day long. One day I heard a wagon passing along the road and I walked over to the fence only to find it was a Mexican who could not speak English. Nevertheless I was glad to see him. Another day my only visitor was a bob cat who passed through the orchard a short distance from where I was working.

In the summertime when the folks were home it was a nice place to be, but in the winter it was very dull. I liked the folks but there was no future in this position and I felt it was time to get back into the seed and nursery business for which I had been trained.

In January of 1896 I left the ranch. I had saved a little money so was not in a hurry to find a job. I made my headquarters, part of the time in Santa Ana and part of the time in Hollywood. I had not had an opportunity to see anything of Southern California so took a few trips visiting Pomona, Ontario, Redlands, Riverside, San Bernardino, Santa Monica, Ventura, Santa Barbara and a few other places. In Ventura I was offered a job with the Theodosia B. Shepherd Nursery but it was not very attractive so I turned it down. In Santa Barbara I was offered a gardener's position on the Whitehead place but it was no better than the one I had just left. Then I heard that John Franklyn, the flower seedsman at Germain's was leaving and going to Australia. I applied for this position and went to work there on April 16th. I was with this firm for seven years and held the position of manager the last year.

In 1903 I started in business for myself at 440 S. Broadway where I had a seed store and nursery yard. In the fall of 1905 I moved to 345 S. Main Street.

I saw Madame Modjeska occasionally and whenever she played in Los Angeles I availed myself of the opportunity of seeing her on the stage, so I saw her in many of her plays.

I spent a weekend on the ranch as a guest of Madame and her husband. We had a very pleasant time and I was glad to see the place again. It had not changed very much. They had added a small area to the garden and built a pool. Also they bought the Harding Canyon and built a dam in the creek so there was a better water supply than when I was there. A Mr. and Mrs. Kelly were also guests there at this time. They were very nice folks and I enjoyed meeting them very much. Mr. Kelly had something to do with Madame's company, I don't know exactly what.

Madame was not at all bashful about telling her age for I remember at the dinner table, somehow the subject of ages came up and Madame said, "I am sixty-three and Charlie (she pronounced it Sharlie) is sixty-one."

I remember they told a rather amusing story at Charlie's expense. It seems Madame was here in California and the Kellys were back east. Mr. Kelly was to come out here in the fall. Madame had a guitar in the east and thought she would like to have it out here. Mr. Bozenta did much of his business by telegrams instead of writing. He spoke several languages and had a good knowledge of English, but sometimes got things a little twisted. What he intended to say in his telegram was, "Send Madame's guitar with Kelly," instead he said, "Send Kelly with Madame's guitar." So here came Kelly clear from back east with this guitar. When he arrived, Mr. Bozenta said, "Kelly, what on earth are you doing out here?" Kelly said, "I don't know. All I know, I was told to leave at once for California with this guitar."

I have very pleasant recollections of this visit to the ranch, which, I think must have been in 1904.

One Sunday morning, I think it was in 1908, I went down town to my store at 345 South Main Street to attend to a few matters which had come up during the week. I remember I was re-arranging the flower seed display near the front of the store when in walked Madame Modjeska. She had been to mass at St. Vibiana's Cathedral at Second and Main Streets. She stayed and chatted for awhile, then left for her hotel. That was the last time I was ever to see Madame Helena Modjeska. She died April 8, 1909, and her remains were taken back to Poland and buried in Cracow, the city of her birth.

She was a great artist, a good woman and one of the most charming persons I have ever known.

✧ *Chapter IX* ✧

BRIEF SKETCH OF LIFE OF MADAME MODJESKA

HELENA MODJESKA was born at Cracow, Poland, on October 12, 1840, being one of a family of ten children. Her father was Michael Opid, a High School teacher of Cracow. He was passionately fond of music and played several instruments. He died when Helena was seven years old. Her three half brothers, Joseph, Simon, and Felix Benda, with four or five young students formed a private theatrical party and gave performances for their friends.

In 1850 Joseph Benda introduced his mother to Mr. Gustave Modjeski (Gustave Sinnmayer Modrzejewski). At that time Helena was ten years old, Modjeski nearly thirty. He became a frequent visitor at the home and used to read to them in the evenings, then have them read in turn. In this way they spent many pleasant evenings. He undertook to teach them German, which was compulsory in the schools. Later Joseph Benda went to Russian Poland and joined a theatrical company. Simon Benda went to Vienna to a conservatory of music, while Felix at nineteen became an actor at the Cracow Theatre.

Felix Benda offered to help Helena go on the stage. He took her to recite before a lady who made a profession of training girls for the theatre. After her first lesson this lady told Helena's brother she had no talent and to tell her mother to keep her home.

The next year Fritz Devrient appeared at the local theatre in *Hamlet* and some other Shakespearian plays. Helena became very interested so Mr. Modjeski secured some Polish translations of Shakespeare, including *Hamlet, The Merchant of Venice* and some others. She recited before Mr. Modjeski and he was quite impressed. He provided her with books and she read with him, Goethe, Wieland, and Lessing. It was during one of these readings that he asked her to marry him.

In 1861, with their young son Rudolphe, they were living in Bochnia, famous for its salt mines. An accident occurred in which a number of men were killed. A benefit was arranged for the widows and orphans. A drama and a farce were produced in the Casino Hall. Mr. Loboiko from Cracow played the part of the leading man while Helena had the leading feminine role. She made a great hit and played to full houses. In the audience was Mr. Checinski, a well known actor of the Warsaw Theatre. He was greatly impressed and hoped, he said, to see her soon in Warsaw. Her doubts were now dispelled. She knew she wanted to become a Polish actress and play in the Imperial Theatre in Warsaw.

Mr. Modjeski persuaded Mr. Loboiko to go to Cracow and obtain a license for a traveling theatrical company. Thus was started a traveling company under the management of Mr. Modjeski. They traveled from place to place in a mountaineer's wagon. Other actors and actresses joined the company and it grew to thirty-six members. They received no regular salaries but divided the receipts. Madame Modjeska was the star from the beginning.

In the spring of 1865 a great sorrow came into her life for she lost both her little daughter and her husband. After this she went to live with her married brother, Felix Benda, in Cracow.

In September of 1865 she signed a contract with the Cracow theatrical management. Her brother Felix was a member of the same company.

On the 12th of September, 1868, she married Count Karol Bozenta Chlapowski, a member of one of the oldest families of the nobility of Poland. Though born in Poland, he was raised and educated in France. Returning to Poland when a young man, he took part in the revolution of 1863, was captured by the Germans and spent twenty months in a German prison.

The day after their marriage Madame and her husband left for Warsaw where she had been offered an engagement at Warsaw Imperial Theatre.

The Warsaw Imperial Theatre was run entirely as a stock company. It was a powerful machine, controlled and subsidized by the Russian government. A new president, Count Serguis Mouchanoff, had been appointed who desired to bring new life into the theatre. Mr. Checinski spoke to him about Madame Modjeska whom he had first seen playing at a benefit in Bochnia and later in the theatre at Cracow. This resulted in her engagement for twelve performances.

Now, certain elements were opposed to any outside talent coming to the theatre and they planned and schemed to discredit this new actress. Included in the repertoire she had chosen for this engagement was *Adrienne Lecouvreur*, considered to be a very difficult play. Many actresses had failed in it. This was to be the last play of the engagement but some scheming people, on some pretext or other, had the schedule changed so that it was booked for the opening night. Thus they hoped to dispose of this new actress at the start. Her friend, Mr. Checinski, sensing what was in the wind, advised her not to show her talent at the rehearsals, but to play the part poorly. This she did and her enemies were well satisfied that she would meet her Waterloo at the very first performance. But they were to be disappointed. The performance she gave before the footlights was entirely different to that at the rehearsals. She received a tremendous ovation, six curtain calls and applause, and applause, and more applause.

Those who had been against her, now acknowledged her as a really great artist and accepted her warm-heartedly. Her reputation was now established as one of the great actresses of Europe and the Warsaw Imperial Theatre offered her a contract at a good salary.

She played an extra engagement with the Warsaw Theatre and signed a contract to go into effect as soon as her present contract with the Cracow Theatre expired.

On the 28th of April, 1869, her work in her native city being finished, she and her husband left for Warsaw. At Warsaw they soon surrounded themselves with a group of artists, musicians and writers. Their house became the meeting place for a circle of talented, intellectual personalities. It was at one of these meetings that she first met Henry K. Sienkiewicz, who later was to become the author of *Quo Vadis*.

Ludwig Grossman was the owner of the foremost musical house in Warsaw. Besides being the proprietor of one of the largest piano concerns in Poland and Russia he was a great musician and composer himself. It was at his house that Madame first met Anton Rubinstein, Hans von Bulow, and other great musicians of that time.

A number of circumstances led up to Madame Modjeska and her friends deciding to come to America. Madame was in poor health and the doctor recommended a rest and a sea voyage. The Centennial Exposition was soon to open in Philadelphia and her son Rudolphe was very anxious to see this; Sienkiewicz and others talked and dreamed of life in a new country.

Madame's husband, Mr. Bozenta, conceived the idea of forming a small Polish colony in California. Those who joined in the movement besides Madame and her family were Henry K. Sienkiewicz, Jules Sypniewski, his wife and two children, and Lucian Paprocki.

In July, 1876, the party sailed for New York where they spent a few weeks making frequent trips to Philadelphia to visit the Centennial Exposition. From New York the party sailed for California by way of Panama. A few days out from New York an explosion in the boiler room killed two men and crippled the ship. The two sailors had to be buried at sea and the ship towed back to New York. After a delay of a few weeks the party again sailed for Panama. They crossed the isthmus and boarded a ship for San Francisco. Here they were welcomed by a group of Polish people who had heard of their coming. The party had decided on Anaheim for their home as they understood it was a German colony and they could all speak the German language. Jules Sypniewski, with his family, left at once for Anaheim to look for a ranch for their new home.

Edwin Booth was then playing at the California Theatre in San Francisco and Madame Modjeska had the pleasure of seeing him in *Shylock* and *Marc Antony*. She was greatly impressed by his acting. Little did she dream then that years later she would be co-starring with this greatest of American actors.

After a short stay in San Francisco the party left for Anaheim where Sypniewski had already secured a ranch. The house on this ranch was very small with only two bedrooms, so Sienkiewicz and Paprocki had to sleep in a room fitted up in the barn.

The men were full of enthusiasm when they went out one morning to work in the orange grove. At night they were tired but still cheerful. However, the next morning some were late for breakfast and a day or so later they developed back aches and other ailments. After about a week the only ones still working were Madame's husband and her son. None of these idealists had any practical experience in farming. Their dream of a paradise in sunny California was rapidly falling to pieces. They were homesick and disillusioned. Still, there were some compensations. There were a number of saddle horses on the ranch and they enjoyed riding around the country. Also they could go out anytime and shoot quail or cottontails and sometimes wild ducks for the dinner table.

One day a man and his wife stopped and chatted with Madame and her husband. This couple was Mr. and Mrs. J. E. Pleasants, who had a home in the Santiago Canyon and who, before leaving, extended an invitation to visit them there. This chance meeting was to have a great influence on the future life of Madame Modjeska and her family.

The end of the year found Mr. Bozenta and Madame in financial difficulties, they having dropped a considerable amount of money in this idealistic venture. It was then decided that Madame should go to San Francisco and study English with the view of appearing on the American stage.

In January of 1877, Madame Modjeska left for San Francisco where she stayed with some Polish friends. It was here, a little later, that Madame had the good fortune to meet Miss Josephine Tuholsky who undertook to give her free lessons in English. Miss Tuholsky became a lifelong friend and it was largely due to her patience and perseverance that Madame Modjeska was able to appear on the American stage. In the meantime, Mr. Bozenta, Rudolphe, Madame's son, and Paprocki went to live in a tiny shack in the mountains about a mile above the home of Mr. and Mrs. J. E. Pleasants in the Santiago Canyon. They used the shack to sleep in, living most of the time out of doors and doing all their cooking under a big live oak tree. They bought what food they could afford and supplemented this diet by hunting quail and cottontails. Their only near neighbor was an old Russian who lived in a log cabin which he had built for himself a little farther up the canyon. They made frequent visits to the Pleasants' home and spent some enjoyable evenings there.

Meanwhile in San Francisco, Madame Modjeska was very much discouraged. She was separated from her husband and her son and she missed them very much. She was hard up for cash and had to dispose of some of her silverware in order to raise a little spending money. The authorities at the California Theatre seemed reluctant to allow her to demonstrate her powers of acting on the stage. In Europe her name was well known but out here no one had ever heard of her. She met with one rebuff after another. She became so despondent she even thought of jumping off the Oakland Ferry, but Josephine Tuholsky was her steadfast friend and was always on hand to cheer her up. Finally, through the intercession of the Governor of California and a few other people in San Francisco, her request was granted and she was allowed to demonstrate her acting ability on the stage of the California Theatre. After this one performance she could have anything she wanted.

Mr. John McCullough, the leading actor at the California Theatre in San Francisco, asked Madame how she spelled her name. She thereupon wrote it down and handed it to him. "Helena Modrzejewska." He said, "Who on earth could ever pronounce that? We will have to change it." Thus, by leaving out some of the letters the name "Modjeska" was coined. It was easy to pronounce and had a nice sound. Madame's son, Rudolphe, who had now come to join his mother in San Francisco, decided to change his name to Ralph Modjeski.

Madame Modjeska made her first appearance on the American stage at the California Theatre in San Francisco in *Adrienne Lecouvreur*. It was a tremendous success and the press gave glowing reports of this new Polish actress. The next day she signed a contract with Mr. Harry Sargent, a theatrical agent, for a tour of the east beginning with New York. As this tour would not start until December she played for a time at the California Theatre in San Francisco and also appeared in other towns in California and Nevada.

In December, 1877, Madame Modjeska made her first appearance in New York in *Adrienne Lecouvreur* at the Fifth Avenue Theatre, which remained on the bills for three weeks. Then, in January, 1878, this was followed by *Camille* which made a great hit. Her entirely new and refined version of *Camille* met with great favor among the people of New York and established her reputation there. After the first performance, her manager informed her there was not a single seat left for that week and that they were selling tickets for the following week.

From New York, she went to Philadelphia and then to Boston where she met Henry W. Longfellow and was invited to visit him at his home in Cambridge. Thus a friendship started that continued until the time of the poet's death. While in Boston her husband arrived from California, having sold the ranch and arranged for the return of the Sypniewski family to Poland. Paprocki, the cartoonist, decided to stay in this country and try to get a job with a newspaper.

From Boston Madame Modjeska went to Washington. Here she met General Grant and General Sherman. Baltimore, Louisville and Chicago were visited next where she played to full houses.

In the summer of 1878 Madame Modjeska, together with her son and her husband, boarded a steamer for Ireland. After a visit to Killarney Lakes, Blarney Castle and Dublin they crossed over to England. From England they went to Poland to visit their relatives and then to Paris to see the Exposition and buy new dresses. In Paris she had the pleasure of seeing Sarah Bernhardt on the stage for the first time at the Theatre Francais.

Madame's son, Ralph, decided he wanted to become a civil engineer so she made arrangements for him to remain in Paris and attend the School of Bridges and Roads.

The season of 1878-79 Madame Modjeska opened at the Fifth Avenue Theatre in New York, after which she toured the country. As many of the towns were one night shows, Madame could not get sufficient rest. Mr. Sargent conceived the idea of her traveling in a private car. Thus she was the first actress in America to travel this way.

In April, 1879, Madame Modjeska made her second visit to Boston, playing in *Adrienne Lecouvreur, Camille,* and *Romeo and Juliet.* After the performance of the last she met Mr. and Mrs. James T. Fields, Oliver Wendell Holmes, Edwin Booth and some other celebrities. At these performances, the Globe Theatre was so packed there was not even standing room.

On May 1, 1880, Madame Modjeska made her London debut at the Court Theatre in *Heartsease.*

This was a new title for *Camille.* It was a tremendous success. The Prince of Wales (later King Edward VII) called to offer his congratulations. Among others who called were Sarah Bernhardt and Henry Irving. This play ran continuously until the first of July.

The next season Madame Modjeska played again in London, this time appearing in *Marie Stuart* which ran for nearly one hundred performances. After one of these, Ellen Terry, the famous English actress, called to offer her congratulations.

In December *Marie Stuart* was followed by *Adrienne Lecou-*

vreur and later in the season by *Romeo and Juliet*. During this season Madame Modjeska and her husband met at social functions many celebrated people of that time including Robert Browning, Lord Leighton, Laurenz Alma Tadema, the great Dutch painter, Labouchere, Bret Harte and some others. They spent a few days as the guests of Alfred Tennyson at his country home "Hazelmere" in Surrey. After this they went to Paris for a few weeks during which time they were invited to meet Victor Hugo.

In September of 1882 Madame and her husband sailed for New York where they met her manager Mr. Stetson, who arranged her repertoire for the season as follows: *Adrienne Lecouvreur, Camille, Romeo and Juliet, Marie Stuart, Frou-Frou, As You Like It,* and *Twelfth Night.*

In the summer of 1883 Madame Modjeska with her son and her husband returned to California and went to visit the Pleasants in the Santiago Canyon. Ralph was eager to show his mother the shack where they lived for a time while she was in San Francisco studying English. They had a very enjoyable time and were enchanted with the beauty of this place.

Madame and her husband made several trips to Poland where she appeared on the stage at Cracow, Warsaw, Posen and Lemberg. They also spent some time at a villa they had built at Zakopane in the Tetra Mountains. Here they met for the first time Ignace Paderewski, then a young man of eighteen.

After playing at the Lyceum Theatre in London in 1884, Madame Modjeska crossed over to Ireland and appeared on the stage in Dublin, receiving a warm welcome from the Irish people.

Ralph Modjeski, having completed his studies in Paris, in 1885, married his cousin Felicie Benda. In September of the same year, Madame Modjeska, her husband, together with Ralph and his bride, two maids and a little mountain boy, ten years old, later known as Johnnie Hare, all sailed for America. They came on to California and went to visit the Pleasants in the Santiago Canyon. A little later Madame purchased the ranch from Mr. Pleasants and built the present house. She loved this place and named it "Forest of Arden." After this they usually spent a few months there each summer.

Lawrence Barrett was Edwin Booth's manager and he made Madame Modjeska an offer to co-star with Mr. Booth. Thus America's greatest actor and actress were brought together on the same stage. They appeared in many different plays and this was one of the most successful seasons in Madame's career.

Madame Modjeska played one season with Otis Skinner as her leading man and another season as co-stars. In 1901 and 1902 she co-starred with Louis James in *Henry VIII, Marie Stuart, Macbeth* and *The Merchant of Venice.*

Madame Modjeska had a long and successful career on the American stage, making her last appearance in 1907. She had a brilliant mind, a knowledge of several languages and a wonderful memory, making it possible for her to memorize a part on short notice. Perhaps her greatest gift was her ability to transfer herself for the time being, into the character she was portraying on the stage. She really felt she was living the part. I once heard her say that it affected her whole life. If she were playing a pleasing part she would feel happy and gay all day, but if it were a sad part she felt sad and depressed.

Note: Much of the foregoing history was obtained from Madame Modjeska's own writings. See "Memories and Impressions of Helena Modjeska," published by the Macmillan Company in 1910.

LIFE ON THE MODJESKA RANCH

IN THE GAY NINETIES

by

THEODORE PAYNE

Dust jacket from first edition of Life on the Modjeska Ranch in the Gay
Nineties *(1962)*

Helena Modjeska as Mary Stuart, c. 1884

*Helena Modjeska
as Magda, c. 1894*

*Charles Bozenta Chlapowski,
Modjeska's husband, c. 1894*

*Theodore Payne while he was employed at the Modjeska Ranch,
c. 1894*

Front of the Modjeska house designed by Stanford White, with the well at the left

Modjeska house and rose garden, with the dog Oso

Cook house and bunk house at Modjeska Ranch, with Theodore Payne on his horse Frank

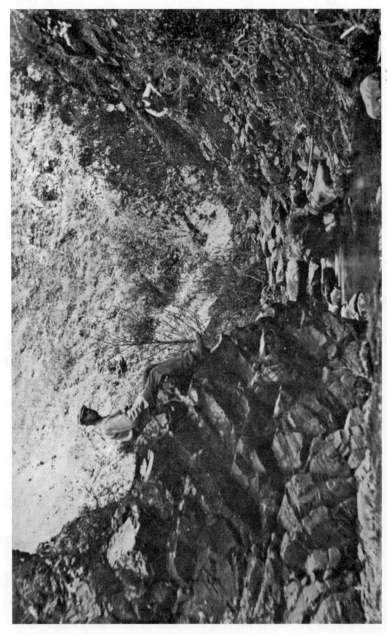

Santiago Canyon above the Modjeska home, c. 1895, Theodore Payne at left. This area is now part of the Modjeska Wilderness Preserve in Orange County.

Helena Modjeska seated at the fountain, c. 1901

Rose Garden at Arden, containing many old-fashioned varieties, c. 1902

Madame Modjeska at the well

Adventures among the Southern California Plants

Wild Cucumber - *Echinocystis fabacea.*

The Hitch Hiker

Billy Clatworthy was from Cornwall, the southernmost county of England. A little fellow, not more than five feet three inches tall, I should say, of light complexion with sandy hair and blue eyes. I first met Billy on the Modjeska Ranch where he had come to visit Mr. Ruopp, the ranch foreman and his wife. He stayed a couple of days and I became pretty well acquainted with him. He spoke the dialect peculiar to that part of England and many people had difficulty in understanding him, but I had no such trouble.

Billy lived in an area between Santa Ana and the coast, then known as "The Swamp." It was saltgrass pasture land with lots of willows, and he had cattle and horses. There was a barn and shack where he lived by himself. He invited me to come and stay with him when I should come to Santa Ana, so the next time I went to town I rode out to his place. I had no difficulty in finding the place but there was nobody around. I went to the nearest neighbor's place to see if anyone there knew where Billy had gone. I found the place occupied by a man named Arnold, a remittance man from England. I met him a number of times later in Los Angeles. A decent kind of chap but rather fond of the bottle. Arnold said Billy had probably gone to Santa Ana and would no doubt be back soon. He told me to just go in and make myself at home, so I did that. I put my horse in the barn, fed her and went into the house. It was now suppertime so I rustled up something to eat. After supper I sat around for awhile, then found something, to read. Eight o'clock came and no sign of Billy, then nine, then ten. I was now getting rather sleepy so I decided to go to bed. I had been asleep probably two hours when I woke up. There was a light in the room and I heard a voice say, "Who's here? I saw your horse in the barn but did not know whose it was."

The next day Billy showed me his livestock. This was the first saltgrass pasture I had seen and I was surprised to see the animals looking so well. This pasture was entirely different than in the mountains and there was feed here when the mountain feed had all gone.

In the summer of 1895 John Ruopp left the Modjeska Ranch and in the late fall went to work for the American Beet Sugar Company at Chino. He bought some lumber and put up a one room temporary shack to live in.

I left the Modjeska Ranch in January of 1896 and was staying in Santa Ana when Mr. Ruopp secured a job for Billy at the Sugar factory in Chino. Billy arranged to have his sister and brother in law take over his place while he was away.

Billy wanted to take some of his belongings and furniture to Chino so he could set up housekeeping for himself there. He planned to take a wagon and team and asked me if I would go along and being the team back. I told him I would be glad to do so. We planned to go on Friday and I was to bring the team back on Sunday. Billy was to pick me up in Santa Ana at 8 o'clock in the morning. I was ready on time but no sign of Billy. I waited all morning but he did not come. I had my lunch and had just about come to the conclusion that he had had to postpone the trip for some reason or other when here comes Billy with his wagon and team. It was now past 1 o'clock and a long trip ahead of us. I did not like the idea of having to spend the night somewhere by the roadside, especially on a cold night. However we started out, passing through Anaheim and Fullerton. We turned up the Brea Canyon. What a desolate place, mile after mile, not a soul in sight except an occasional sheep herder with a flock of sheep. We met one team soon after we entered the canyon. That was the only one we saw that whole afternoon. It was dark when we got out of the canyon. A little later we came into a small town. Billy said this must be Puente though we found out later it wasn't. It was Spadra.

It was 9 o'clock when we reached Ruopp's one room shack in Chino. I was a little embarrassed at the thought of all of us sleeping in one room, but if they could stand it so could I.

We carried in a mattress for Billy and me to sleep on and some blankets from the wagon and spread them on the floor. When it came time to retire Billy and I went outside while the married folks went to bed and put out the light. Then we went in and undressed in the dark. The next morning we got up early and went outside so as to give the other folks a chance to get up. Mrs. Ruopp cooked breakfast for all of us, bacon and eggs, toast and coffee, and it tasted real good.

I spent Saturday at Chino then on Sunday morning I started back to Santa Ana with the wagon and team. Billy had brought a little dog with him and now decided to send it back with me which was somewhat of a nuisance.

When passing through Pomona a man with a bundle of blankets on his back asked me for a ride. He wanted to go to Puente so I let him get up on the wagon. When we came to the next town I said, "Well, here you are, this is Puente." "Oh no," said he, "This is Spadra." "Well, then," I said, "I must be mistaken, so I won't be going as far as Puente after all, so you had better get off here. Perhaps you can get a ride with someone else for the rest of the way. I have to go down Brea Canyon to Santa Ana." He said, "You can't get through there now, the road is closed." "I just came through there the day before yesterday," I told him.

When we came to the place where the road turns off for Brea Canyon, he was very insistent and even tried to take the reins out of my hands. He said, "Maybe I should go to Santa Ana. Is there any work to be had there?" I said "No, the streets there are lined with the unemployed."

He was a big fellow and awfully tough looking and I did not like the prospect of that long ride through that desolate country with him. He could bump me off and throw my body in a ravine and I would never be heard of again. Just then a man came along with a horse and cart and the fellow asked him the best way to get to Puente. The man said to walk right along the railroad track would be the nearest way. They talked some more and my passenger got down off the wagon. I did not wait a minute but started up the team and was off. This was one time when I preferred to be alone. I looked back and the man with the horse and cart had picked up the other fellow and was evidently going to drive him somewhere. I said, "You are welcome to him. At least you are driving in a civilized section while I am going into a desolate country."

Brea Canyon today is a very different place with a fine highway passing through it and lots of traffic and development.

Santa Barbara in 1896

In the latter part of March, 1896, I made my first visit to Santa Barbara. Leaving Los Angeles on the morning train I stopped off at Ventura and called on Mrs. Theodosia B. Shepherd who had a nursery on Main Street. She had quite a collection of begonias, phyllocactus (epiphyllums) cacti and rare plants and specialized in growing fringed petunia seed. She published a rather interesting catalog and did a mail order business, using the title and address of "Theodosia B. Shepherd, Rare Plants and Seeds, Ventura-by-the-Sea, California".

She offered me work in the nursery with a small room on the corner of the property to live in. I went to see the old Mission and looked around the town. Then, in the evening, I took a walk up the Avenue for about a mile. I rather liked this little place and was really tempted to accept Mrs. Shepherd's offer, but the pay was not enough.

I stayed the night at the Anacapa Hotel and the next morning boarded the train for Carpinteria where I went to see the "Big Grape Vine," said to be the largest in the world, though there may be some doubt about this. However, it covered an immense area and was visited by many tourists who bought colored post cards to mail to their friends.

I also visited the Fithian Ranch, quite an interesting place, then I caught a later train for Santa Barbara.

In Santa Barbara I found a nursery on State Street just below Victoria Street belonging to John Spence, an Englishman who before coming to this country had worked at Kew Gardens. I remember there was a fine specimen of the South African Silver

Tree (*Leucadendron argenteum*) in the grounds, the first one I had ever seen.

John Spence was a very pleasant fellow with a blonde beard. He told me Whitehead in Montecito was looking for a man and arranged for me to meet him. The next day was Sunday. I hired a saddle horse from a livery stable and rode out Valley Road, then turned up Sycamore Canyon Road to the Whitehead place. Mr. Whitehead was waiting for me among some live oak trees on top of the hill. We had a long talk but the job was no better than the one I had recently left at Madame Modjeska's so I did not take it. This Whitehead place afterwards became the Knapp Estate.

Sunday afternoon and evening I spent at John Spence's home on Modoc Road. It was a pretty home with large grounds and we sat out of doors all afternoon in the shade of some beautiful trees. This was a typical English home and family, John Spence, his wife and two daughters. There was also a son but he was away on a trip to the Santa Ynez Mountains. It was like being back in England and I enjoyed it immensely.

I went to see the old Mission and then spent a little while in the grounds of the Arlington Hotel. This was the original Arlington Hotel, later a new attractive building designed by Arthur Benton of Los Angeles took the place of the old one. This building was wrecked by the earthquake. I remember there was a plant of *Dracaena draco* (Dragon Blood) from the Canary Islands, about ten feet high; this was incorrectly named Joshua Tree (*Yucca arborescens*). I have since wondered why, with so many trained horticulturalists in Santa Barbara, anyone ever came to make such a mistake as to label this plant Joshua Tree. Just thirty years later I was there when this tree had grown into a large specimen and was being boxed to be moved by Otto Niedermuller to the Alameda Plaza.

The next morning I took the train to Goleta where I visited the Joseph Sexton Nursery. Besides a large collection of ornamental stock, pampas grass was grown here by the acre for the dried plumes which was quite an industry in those days.

Many rare plants and trees were planted in the grounds of the Joseph Sexton home. These have since grown into large specimens.

From Goleta I went by train to Ellwood Station to visit the Ellwood Cooper ranch. Ellwood Cooper came to Santa Barbara in 1870 and bought this ranch. He became interested in growing eucalyptus and by 1875 had 50,000 trees growing. He was also a pioneer in the olive industry. Mrs. Cooper took a great interest in her garden and had many rare plants.

Mr. and Mrs. Cooper were delightful people and I enjoyed meeting them very much. I visited this place on a number of occasions in later years and Fanny Cooper, one of the daughters, collected seed of various kinds of eucalyptus for me.

LAUREL CANYON

One Sunday I was walking in Laurel Canyon when I saw a wild flower on the hillside that interested me. I started to climb up the bank; it was very steep and I had to pull myself up by means of the chaparral. When I had climbed 20 or perhaps 30 feet, I came to a ledge about two feet wide which had been cut for a pipe line of a water system, long since abandoned. There, right before me, on this ledge was a rattlesnake! It tried to go down a hole but the hole was not very deep and about half the snake was left outside. I took hold of it and tried to pull it out of the hole but it was slippery and I could not get a good grip. In my pocket I had some small cotton seed bags. I took one of these and wrapped it around the snake so as to get a better hold. Then I gave one, quick jerk, pulling the snake out of the hole and flinging it backwards so that it fell on the road below. When I got down to the road, there was the maddest snake you ever saw, full of fight. I cut a good long stick and killed the snake. It was very broad, a little less than three feet in length, and dark colored. I think sometimes these are called black rattlesnakes. It had a beautiful skin so I took it back to the city with me and skinned it.

It would have been unfortunate if anyone had been passing at the time the snake landed on the road. But very few people went there in those days, and there was only one house in Laurel Canyon at that time.

Lost in the Mountains

The summer of 1900 I spent my vacation at Seven Oaks in the San Bernardino Mountains. At that time, there was no road into Seven Oaks—you went by means of stage from Redlands to Skinner's Ranch, a distance of fifteen miles. Lunch was provided at Skinner's then a ten mile horse back ride over the trail brought you to Seven Oaks in the Santa Ana Canyon. A burro train carried in supplies, guests' baggage and mail.

At Seven Oaks, I met a young man named McIntyre who was also from Los Angeles and we went on several trips together. One day, we took saddle horses and rode ten miles up the Canyon to Big Meadows. We stayed there perhaps an hour, then went on six miles further up the canyon. We tied our horses to a tree then climbed up onto a ridge. This ridge led to a small peak and I thought I would like to climb to the top and get the view. McIntyre said he was not much good at mountain climbing so he would sit down under a pine tree and wait for me.

When I got to the top of the peak, there was another one just like it a little further on. So I climbed to the top of it, then there was another and another and another. I must have climbed at least six or seven of these peaks. From the top of the last one I got a wonderful view looking out onto the desert. I then realized I had come much further than I intended and should be getting back to McIntyre. Instead of climbing to the top of each peak, I thought I could save time by skirting around them; that was where I made my mistake. Pretty soon, I passed a fallen log, a little later I came to another one just like it, then another. I thought it strange there should be so many fallen logs so much alike. It was getting late and I began to travel faster. I tripped and fell over a rock, striking my side. 1 thought it was just a slight bruise and did not pay much attention to it.

Soon I came to the fallen log again. Then I was sure it was the same one and I realized I was lost and was simply going around in a circle. Late in the afternoon, lost and miles from camp, not a situation to feel very cheerful about, I knew I must find some way to get my bearings, so I climbed to the top of the nearest peak. There was old Greyback on my left, just the way it had been all the way from Seven Oaks. If Greyback was on my left coming, it should be to the right going back, so I was facing in exactly the wrong direction. I turned completely around, then picked out what I thought should be the next peak and climbed to the top of it. From there I picked out the next one and climbed it, then the next and so on until I came to a long ridge. I was not sure whether it was the ridge where I had left McIntyre or not, but it looked something like it and I followed along the ridge and began to call. There was no answer, and I was afraid I was on the wrong ridge. Then I started to descend into the canyon, all the time calling. About half way down there was an answer. McIntyre had gotten tired of sitting under the pine tree and had gone down to where the horses were tied. It was now after four o'clock, sixteen miles from camp and my side was hurting badly. We started for home and I found I could not stand traveling faster than the horses could walk. The horse McIntyre rode was exceedingly slow, if he went in the lead and set the pace we would never get home, so I had to go first. My horse was a fine animal, sired by Black Diamond, but had been raised in the valley and was not used to mountain trails. Every little while he would get off the trail so I had to keep a close watch on him. I never will forget that ride. It seemed as though we never would reach camp.

I was in great pain and now realized I had an internal injury. It was after eight o'clock when we reached Seven Oaks. The dining room and kitchen were closed, but Mr. Spourt, the manager, took us into the kitchen and started to make some coffee. I sat down in a chair and a few minutes later passed out. They took me to my cabin and sent for old Dr. Mack who lived a little further up the canyon. He was quite a character who had been a doctor but was now running a sort of saloon or blind pig.

People called him occasionally in emergency cases. Dr. Mack did not do very much for me. I think he gave me some peppermint or something and told them to keep putting hot compresses on me all night. A boy who was working there as a dishwasher volunteered to stay with me so a cot was moved into my cabin for him. He kept the fire going and a kettle of hot water on the stove. Every little while he would get up and put another hot compress on me. All I had to do was to call him and he was up in a minute. No trained nurse could have taken better care of me. I slept very little that night but must have dozed off in the morning, as I did not hear him when he left the cabin.

I asked to see him a little later and was told he had left the camp that morning. I felt very disappointed because I wanted to tell him how much I appreciated his kindness in caring for me.

Mr. LeBas, the proprietor of the camp, came in to see me. He had heard of the accident and was quite concerned. He said Dr. Allen of Redlands was camping in Bear Valley and he would send over and get him. So a little later, Dr. Allen arrived. He examined me and said I had an injured spleen. He bound me up and left instructions for my care. In the camp was an old woman who was hired to care for the LeBas baby and she was given the job of looking after me also.

I was in bed for four or five days, then got up. I was still sore but could walk a little, very slowly. I lay around camp for another four or five days, then asked for a saddle horse to see if I could stand the ride over the trail. I found I could ride if I took it slowly. So two days later I left the camp and returned to Los Angeles. My vacation was over. I had been away over three weeks instead of the two I had planned.

It was a vacation I shall not forget.

A WILD RIDE TO OVERTAKE
A STAGE COACH

In the summer of 1901 I spent my vacation at Idylwild in the San Jacinto Mountains. I had a wonderful time, making several side trips including an overnight one to the top of Mount San Jacinto. There were five of us in the party including the guide who furnished the saddle horses. We climbed the Torquitz Trail, passing through a lot of beautiful country including Round Valley and Long Valley and camped for the night in a beautiful green meadow not far from the summit. We had plenty of blankets but it was so cold we could not sleep well. We arose early in the morning. It was the fifth day of September and the ground was white with frost.

After partaking of a good breakfast we started for the top of the peak which we reached about 8 o'clock. The view was magnificent looking down onto Beaumont, Banning and the Colorado desert. The Eucalyptus trees in Beaumont looked like little rows of lettuce and a train coming up the grade from Indio like a caterpillar crawling along.

While at Idylwild, I collected quite a number of flowers and one immense cone of the Coulter Pine which I carried for five miles, strapped to my saddle. This is one of the largest I have ever seen. I have it to this day.

My vacation over, it was now time to return to Los Angeles so I notified the office that I would be leaving on the stage the next morning. My baggage was loaded on the stage and I was promised a call when ready to start. Somehow this failed and the stage left without me.

Dr. Walter Lindley was at Idylwild at the time. I think he was the president or general manager of the company. He and his little grandson and a nurse were leaving in a few minutes for Hemet in a buckboard. He told me I might ride with them. Dr. Lindley and the nurse sat in the front seat while the little boy and I occupied the back seat. The doctor was a wild driver and it seemed to me we went around some of the curves on one wheel. We had to hang on for dear life and the hind wheels wobbled terribly. The one on my side cut the back of my hand leaving a scar I have to this day.

After going two or three miles the double-tree broke leaving us stranded by the roadside. There was very little traffic on the road in those days and not much likelihood of anyone coming along. Dr. Lindley asked, "Can you ride?" "Yes" I said, "I can ride." "Well," he said, "You take one of these horses and see if you can catch up with the stage. It is not far ahead." I picked out the horse with the best shaped back, took the harness off, fixed a piece of rope to the bridle and mounted my steed. It was not very comfortable riding bare-back down a steep grade, especially on a winding mountain road.

Sometimes, I had to slow up, then I would strike a piece of good road and would make better time. Soon I sighted the stage, but try as I would I could not catch up with it. The horse did the best he could but he was no race horse. I waved at the people on the stage and they waved back but showed no signs of stopping. In fact, the more I waved the faster the stage seemed to go. I think they got the idea I was trying to outrun them and the stage driver speeded up. It was a long ride from where the buckboard broke down to Hemet, but I made it, coming in just about a minute behind the stage.

I told the stage driver what had happened, so, after unloading the baggage, he turned around and went back to pick up the doctor and his party.

The first news I heard upon reaching Hemet was that President William McKinley had been assassinated. There was only one train a day from Hemet in those days so I stayed that night at a hotel and came home to Los Angeles the next day.

A Day on the Desert
Without Water

In the spring of 1903, in company of the late Dr. Anstruther Davidson, I made a botanizing trip to the Colorado desert. At Thermal there was a ranch owned by a Mrs. Green and her son Aden. The house was only a short distance from the railroad track and they made a business of putting up guests. We arranged to stay there.

The next day we took two saddle horses and started out on our trip, intending to go to Torres Canyon. Mrs. Green said she would put us up some lunch and asked what we would like to have. Dr. Davidson said, "We won't need much, just give us some crackers and cheese."

At that time I had half interest in a quarter section of land upon which we had drilled a well and made some other improvements. We stayed there awhile then went on and stopped at two or three other ranches. At the last one we talked with the owner, telling him that we were looking for wild flowers and that we were headed for Torres Canyon. "Why don't you go to Martinez Canyon?" he asked, "You would be more likely to find flowers there and also there is water in that canyon. The first one you see is Torres Canyon, Martinez is over there." He pointed it out in the distance.

We decided to go to Martinez Canyon. Following the edge of the foothills, we passed through an Indian village. We stopped to talk to some of the Indians and noticed that many of them were suffering with sore eyes. There seemed to be some sort of epidemic. Dr. Davidson had practiced medicine in Arizona and was used to treating Indians. He promised to send them something that would cure their sore eyes.

We continued on our way following the edge of the foothills until we came to the mouth of the Martinez Canyon. We found a number of wild flowers, including the beautiful Spotted Mallow (*Malvastrum rotundifolium*), and *Mohavea viscida*, both of which I had not seen before. We continued up the canyon for quite a distance but found no sign of water. It was now about 1 o'clock and we were suffering badly for want of something to drink. I left the doctor at this point and went on a little further by myself. I came to a survey monument which read elevation 2500 feet. My ranch, where we had stopped, was 160 feet below sea level so we had climbed considerably.

I went on still further and came to a fall but it was dry. The ground below the fall was barely moist; that was the nearest I came to finding water. I returned to where I had left the doctor and told him the bad news. He said, "You had better not eat any lunch, that would only make you feel worse." I certainly did not want anything to eat, so we never opened our lunch bags but left them tied to the saddles.

We decided to start home and after awhile came to the mouth of the canyon. When you are in the valley it is quite easy to pick out any canyon and go straight for it, but when you come out of a canyon and try to locate a certain spot in the valley, it is entirely different. Of course, we wanted to head for Thermal, and that is where we got into an argument. The doctor said we should go over there and I said no, we should go over here. Well, I let him have his way but felt confident he was wrong. It did not look at all like the country we had come through in the morning and pretty soon we got into an area where the growth was so thick and high we could hardly get through it. "Doctor," I said, "I am sure we are going too far south. There may be a shorter way to Thermal than the way we came but it is safer to turn left and follow along in a line with the foothills. Then we know where we are." We did this and about 5 o'clock we came to a ranch where we quenched our thirst and watered the horses. This was the first drink we had had since about 9:30 that morning. About an hour and a half more ride and we were back at Thermal.

Mrs. Green had a great big dinner prepared for us but we could eat nothing. All we wanted to do was drink tea. The doctor said, "Drink all you want, Payne, it won't hurt you." I am not sure whether he drank seven cups and I drank eight, or he drank eight and I, nine. I know I got the best of him by one cup.

After we had related our experiences, Mrs. Green said, "Well, if you had opened your lunch bags you would have found oranges in them." Doctor Davidson said, "Payne, come over here and kick me." Said I, "Let's go out to the barn and have the mules kick both of us." He had asked for crackers and cheese and we supposed that was all we had been given. Crackers and cheese are not much use when you are almost dying of thirst. But oranges! Oh my! Of course it was a very foolish thing to go on a trip like that without taking some water along but when we started we had no idea of going so far, and the rancher who had told us about Martinez Canyon said we would find water there, so we did not give it another thought.

I felt very shaky that evening but slept well and was all right in the morning and ready for a good breakfast.

Mrs. Green told Dr. Davidson about a woman in the neighborhood who was sick and he went off to see what he could do to help her. He was like that. Always doing some kind deed for someone. After he got back to Los Angeles he sent Aden Green a supply of boracic acid and told him to take it to the Indian village and instruct the Indians how to use it. This Green did and he told me afterwards that the Indians were soon cured of their sore eyes and were profuse in their praises of the kind doctor who had visited their village and sent them the good medicine.

Two Royal Coffins

In the Readers' Digest a few years ago appeared a very interesting story about four coffins which some American soldiers had found hidden away in an old salt mine in Germany. These coffins contained the remains of Frederick William I, King of Prussia; Frederick the Great, King of Prussia; Paul Von Hindenburg and Frau Von Hindenburg. This story does not concern the latter two but only the royal coffins.

Upon reading this article my thoughts went back to the summer of 1903. I was traveling in Europe, accompanied by Frank Hicks, a cousin of mine. For myself it was primarily a business trip, but for Frank it was just a vacation. After visiting nurseries in Belgium and bulb fields in Holland we were now bound for the seed farms of Germany. As Berlin was on our route we decided to spend a few days there and see the city. On Saturday night we went to a theatre which was located not very far from our hotel. Of course, we did not understand the German language but we could get a pretty good idea of what the play was about and it was interesting to see the people. After the show we started to walk back to our hotel but must have taken a wrong turn somewhere for we soon found ourselves in a strange part of the city. We seemed to be in a more open area and there was a wide avenue of trees. It was very quiet and there was no one around. Eleven o'clock at night and here we were lost in a big city in a foreign country where we could not speak the language. Frank was worried but I said, "We will find our way back somehow." I looked for the nearest street sign and it read "Unter den Linden". So this was the famous avenue of trees. We had seen it before by day light.

I had in my pocket a good map of Berlin so I took this out and with the aid of one of the street lamps I located the spot where we were. Then by carefully checking the streets on the map we were able to find our way back to our hotel in half an hour.

We left Berlin on Sunday bound for Quedlinburg, a small city in the heart of a seed growing district. We arrived there about 5 o'clock in the afternoon. Not knowing the names of any of the hotels in this place, we had to select one from the busses awaiting the arrival of the train. The sign on one of these read "Hotel Zum Bunten Lamm". This name rather intrigued us so we decided to go there. It proved to be a quaint old place but quite comfortable. Upon arrival at the hotel we heard the bus driver tell someone he had brought two Englishmen from the station. Whereupon a waiter appeared who could speak a few words of English. This man was quite a help to us during the next few days.

After the evening meal the waiter came to me, and speaking very slowly said, "You know Mr. Carl Cropp, Chicago?" "Oh yes," I replied. "I know Mr. Carl Cropp." Then he said, "He here." "Oh", I said, "That is fine. Will you please tell him I am here and would like to see him?" Then he replied, "No! He here, he go today Berlin." We had just come from Berlin so we must have passed each other going in opposite directions.

Incidentally, Carl Cropp was vice president of the Vaughan Seed Company of Chicago. I believe at that time he had the reputation of being the best informed flower seeds man in the United States. He was born and raised in the seed business in Germany and could have given me many pointers about the growers of Quedlinburg and Erfurt. I did not see Carl Cropp until three or four years later when, one afternoon, he came into my store on South Main Street. I told him how we had just missed each other over there in Germany in 1903. He remembered the trip and staying at the Hotel Zum Bunten Lamm but, of course, had no idea that I was in that part of the world.

On Monday morning we called on the firm of Dippe Brothers, whom I believe at that time had the reputation of being the largest seed growers in the world. They grew a general line but specialized in vegetable and field seeds. They supplied practically all the sugar beet seed used in California. The man who took us around was named Zander and he spoke good English. In fact all the seed firms we visited in Quedlinburg and later in Erfurt had men who spoke English, also most of the firms published an English edition of their catalogs. We saw vast fields of plants grown for seed, immense drying sheds and warehouses, a long office building with whole rows of people working at desks. One thing that interested us very much were the long rows of stalls filled with tall Bavarian oxen which were used in place of horses.

The next day we visited the old firm of Henry Mette established in 1784, also one of the largest seed growing firms in the world. They had a wonderful collection of flower seeds including some California natives not available anywhere in America.

Then we called on the firms of Frederick Roemer, Martin Grasshoff, David Sacks and some others.

The last day we were in Quedlinburg a man came to the hotel from Dippe Brothers. He said, "You have now probably seen all the seed farms you want to see. How would you like to visit some of the historical parts of this old city?" We told him if he could spare the time we should enjoy it very much.

Quedlinburg is an interesting old city situated on the Bode, near the northwest base of the Harz Mountains in the province of Saxony. It was a fortress of Henry the Fowler about 922.

The Abbey of Quedlinburg was founded by Otto the Great and at one time controlled nearly 40 square miles of territory. In

1539 the people of the town accepted the reformed doctrine and the Abbey was converted into a Protestant sisterhood.

After inspecting the Abbey our guide said, "Down underneath there is a crypt containing some old tapestries, paintings and other objects. If you like I can get the guard to unlock the door for us." We thought we might as well take in everything there was to see so we consented and the guard opened up the door. There were a great many things of interest which I do not now remember. One thing, however, I shall never forget being two coffins. Frederick William I, King of Prussia; and Frederick the Great, King of Prussia. I sat on the coffin of Frederick the Great and read the inscription.

These were the identical coffins which the American soldiers later found hidden away in an old salt mine. They had evidently been removed from Quedlinburg and when the war came along were hidden away in the old salt mine for safety. The article in the Readers' Digest was a rather humorous story. The American authorities had to consult with the present head of the Hohenzollern family as to what disposition to make of these two coffins. The representative of the Hohenzollerns somehow got it into his head that the spokesman for the Americans had come to ask for the hand of his daughter in marriage, instead of which he had come to ask what to do with two old coffins.

The Readers' Digest story was amusing and I felt I had a special interest in these two coffins. It seemed something like hearing from two old acquaintances.

THE OSTRICHES DIDN'T
LAY ENOUGH EGGS

At the time I worked for Germain's, which was from the spring of 1896 to the spring of 1903, this firm carried a stock of ostrich egg shells for the tourist trade. These egg shells were imported from a firm in London. Miss Engelbracht, who worked in Germain's store, used to decorate some of them with paintings. Her favorite subjects were one of the old Missions or a stately California Fan Palm. Shells so decorated sold for $2.50 each while the plain ones sold for $1.50 each.

When I started in business in 1903 I was located at 440 South Broadway, a good location for retail trade. I thought I would like to handle some ostrich egg shells myself, but why buy them in London? Why not get them direct from Africa, thus getting the benefit of a lower price? My friend, West Cove, with his wife and daughter were living in Hollywood. I had known them in England and we came out to this country together. I remembered that Mrs. Cove had brothers in South Africa, so West wrote to one of them in Johannesburg and asked him if he could ship us a quantity of ostrich egg shells. His reply was favorable and a little later a large shipment of those egg shells arrived. I don't remember how many cases there were but there were quite a number of them. There was some loss through breakage in transit, but even at that the cost was much lower than I could have laid them down from London, so that I was able to wholesale them to curio stores in Los Angeles, Pasadena, Redlands, Riverside and other towns at a price so much lower than Germain's that all those stores were glad to lay in a good stock.

The Ostrich Farm in South Pasadena was then in full swing and many tourists took back on ostrich egg shell as a souvenir from the farm. Now it seems that the ostriches there were not laying enough eggs to keep up with the demand of the tourists. Someone told them at the farm that I had a quantity of egg shells and a representative from there came to see me with the result that they bought all I had left, with the exception of a few dozen which I reserved for retail sales.

It was a profitable and interesting venture, but, as every one knows, there is always plenty to do in a Nursery, Seed and Landscape business without going into side lines, so I let it go at that.

Following the Coast in 1904

In the late spring of 1904 accompanied by a friend named P. H. Field, I went on a three day camping trip up the coast from Santa Monica. Field was the owner of a horse and light wagon which served us for transportation. We met by appointment in Santa Monica. Field had the wagon all ready, loaded with camping materials and a supply of water and food for the horse. We went to a store and purchased provisions enough for three days, then started on our trip along the coast. The road was very poor, not much more than a wagon track so we drove much of the time on the beach. We had plenty of time so took it easy, walking sometimes and riding sometimes.

We met a man that Field knew. His name was Henry and he lived in a canyon not far from the beach. He was going into town for a few days and said we might camp on his place if we liked. So we camped there that night under a live oak tree. It was not a very attractive place and it was rather hot. We would really have been better off on the beach.

Perez Hastings Field was quite a character. He loved to camp and cook and would do all the work if you let him. He was probably in his early forties, of medium height, slight build and fair complexion with a blond beard and a soft pleasant voice. He was well educated and trained as an architect, though he never followed the profession. He had lived for five years in Paris where he studied art. He had been on an archeological expedition to Syria or some other country in the middle east for one of our universities, I think it was Pennsylvania but I am not sure.

His mother was well known in literary circles and was the founder of the Twentieth Century Club of New York, of which she was president for many years.

Field worked for me off and on for a number of years, and he soon acquired a good knowledge of the plants and was very helpful in the nursery and with landscaping work. I think he received a small allowance from his mother but he liked to work now and then to add a little to his income. He was not at all ambitious and his wants were very simple. He was, however, well informed on many subjects and I always enjoyed his company.

The next day we continued on up the coast and found a number of wild flowers where there were sand dunes, including two kinds of sand verbena, sun cups, wild heliotrope, bush sunflower and some others. I was particularly interested in seeing how low the chaparral came on the hills facing the ocean. The California holly, mountain mahogany, chamise, wild buckwheat and lemonade berry were especially noticeable, while even yuccas were growing not very far up the slope. There was a very interesting arch rock over the road at one spot. I have been told that the movies blew it up but do not know whether that is true, at any rate it is not there now.

We found a good place to camp that night on the beach. Someone else had camped there and had left a fireplace all ready to use. We were getting ready for supper when we had a visitor, a man who lived in a canyon nearby. We invited him to have supper with us and he stayed and talked for a couple of hours. This was the second person we had seen since leaving Santa Monica. I don't know if this man was lonesome or if it was Field's cooking that attracted him, anyhow, he showed up in time for breakfast the next morning.

The first thing we did upon arising was to take a dip in the ocean. We did not need bathing suits because there was no one to see us except the birds and they did not mind. Then, of course, we had to feed the horse, then cook breakfast; bacon and eggs and coffee never tasted so good.

We met another man that day. He owned a piece of land facing the ocean and including a mesa, which he informed us would make a wonderful building site some day.

After traveling for awhile Field said, "I believe we are now on the Malibu Ranch and we may be stopped and turned back." However, we didn't see a soul. We collected some filaree seed for which I had a demand in those days.

About noon we started to retrace our steps and camped that night on the same spot as the night before, then returned to Santa Monica the next day. Besides the three men mentioned we met just one other, making a total of four people in a little over three days.

Now, as we travel along the Roosevelt Highway, with hundreds of automobiles tearing by, it is hard to believe that this is the same beach that was "all ours" for three wonderful days long years ago.

A Palm Deal

Back in the early part of the century, *Cocos plumosa* (or more correctly *Cocos romanzoffiana*) palms were quite rare in Los Angeles. I think it was in the summer of 1906 I was spending a few days in Santa Barbara when a man in Montecito told me about some of these palms that were for sale at the Show Ranch. I was not particularly interested but before I came home I thought I would investigate the matter so I stopped at the ranch and found a little Danish fellow named Buckendahl in charge. He showed me the palms, there were 24 of them ranging in height from 16 to 22 feet and he had them priced according to size. The prices were for the plants as they stood in the ground, the customer to box and move them. I made a list of the prices and sizes and took it back to Los Angeles with me. Arriving home, I contacted a few people whom I thought might be interested, but without success. Oscar Morris of Morris & Snow Seed thought he had a prospective buyer so I turned the list over to him but he had no success, then Fred Howard had a try at it with the same result so I gave up the project for the time being.

One Saturday evening during the following March, Jacob Dieterich, who had a nursery at 12th and Wall Streets, came into my store on South Main Street. Jake said, "What did you ever do about those Cocos palms you were trying to sell?" I said, "Nothing Jake, I'm just laying low for the time being." "Well," he said, "I believe we could sell them now. I'll tell you what I'll do. If you like, I'll go in the deal with you 50/50. We can put the palms in my nursery. I have a good many wealthy customers." I said, "That's fine, Jake, it's a deal. When do you want to go and see the palms?"

We decided to go to Santa Barbara on Sunday morning a week later. I was to meet him at the Arcade Depot. When the day arrived, it was just pouring with rain but I had promised to meet Jake at the depot so I was there on time. It rained all the way to Santa Barbara but cleared up in the afternoon and then the sun came out. I went to a livery stable and hired a horse and buggy and drove Jake out to the Show Ranch, When he saw the palms his eyes just about popped out of his head. "They are beautiful specimens, we sure can make money out of them!" I said to him, "The way Buckendahl has them priced they total up to $584.00. My idea would be to offer him $500.00 for the lot."

The next morning we rented a horse and buggy and again drove out to the ranch to talk to Buckendahl. I told him we were interested in the palms and would give him $500.00 for the lot. He told us we had better go into Santa Barbara and see Mr. Show at his store. Mr. Show had a high class provision store on State Street and we found him in his office. Show was a rather gruff sort of a person. Buckendahl told him we were interested in buying the palms. He turned to us, "Well! Do you want them?" I said, "That depends, Mr. Show, on what kind of a deal we can make. We are willing to give you $500.00 for the lot, $100.00 down and the balance before we move the palms in June." Show said, "Well, Buckendahl, what do you think about it?" Buckendahl replied, "Well, sir, I think that is a good offer." Show said, "All right." I dictated a short agreement to Show's bookkeeper and we closed the deal.

Later, Jake tried to interest Mr. and Mrs. E. L. Doheny in these palms and we all went up to Santa Barbara together to see them, but we did not make a deal.

In June we arranged with Mr. Peter Riedel of Santa Barbara to box the palms and load them onto a flat car. I found another very good specimen in a private estate. We bought it and added it to the shipment. The flat car arrived in Los Angeles safely and we hired a big truck to haul the palms from the railroad station to Dieterich's nursery at 12th and Wall Streets. Going around the corner at 4th and San Pedro Streets, three of the palms fell off the truck. I received a phone call at my store, and, taking one man with me, went down there immediately. Two of the boxes were not damaged a great deal and we got them back onto the truck without much trouble. The third was broken all to pieces. By the time we had it rolled back onto the truck all the earth on the roots would not fill an ordinary bucket. Jake was terribly upset and thought we would lose it. However, he put it in a box and placed it in the shade of a tree at his own home, just a block from the nursery. It came out all right and just as good as the others.

The palms made a good display in Dieterich's nursery and he had some inquiries but no sales. Jake said, "Don't worry, they will sell." I didn't worry, because I had great confidence in him.

These palms cost us $500.00 plus the boxing, freight and hauling charges, which were about $50.00. Then there were a few miscellaneous expenses like our trips to Santa Barbara.

All told it made a total investment of about $1,000.00 which was not so much, considering the size of the palms.

One day in the following spring a man who owned a large estate in the south part of the city came into Dieterich's nursery. I will call him Mr. X. He said, "Dieterich, what do you want for these four palms?" Jake replied, "One hundred fifty dollars apiece." Mr. X said, "You are crazy, you will never get that much for them. I'll tell you what I'll do. I'll give you $100.00 apiece for them." "No!" said Jake, "The price is $150.00 and nothing less," After Mr. X had left, Jake made four signs, "SOLD", "SOLD",

"SOLD", "SOLD". He put them on the four palms Mr. X had been looking at.

About a week later Mr. X came back, just as Jake knew he would. When he saw the palms he blew up. He said, "Why, Dieterich, you sold my palms! You sold my palms!" Jake said, "Why no, I didn't. You said you didn't want to buy them. Mr. Payne sold them for $200.00 apiece." Mr. X turned right around and selected four others and gave Jake a check for $600.00.

This started it. The gardener from the Kerckhoff place on Adams Street came and took two or three. Judge Silent took one and there were others I don't remember. Then a representative from the Huntington Estate came and took all the rest. In three weeks the palms were all sold.

When Jake and I sat down to figure out how we had come out, we found we had cleared $1810.00 or $905.00 each on the deal. Not a bad investment.

My business was not very good that season and in the meantime I had married and started buying a home, so the money came in very handy.

Stalled in a Tunnel

I think it must have been during the winter of 1905, though I am not sure. I was visiting my friends Mr. and Mrs. John Ruopp on the Patterson Ranch about two miles from Oxnard. It was raining when I arrived there and continued to pour all night and all the next day. There were floods and the railway track was damaged so there were no trains to Los Angeles for a few days. I was stranded with no way to get home. We telephoned to the depot at Oxnard to find out if the trains were running but each day it was the same answer, "No trains today."

Then on the third or fourth day, I am not sure which, they told us a train was being made up consisting of one passenger car and an engine. They hoped to get through to Los Angeles and the train would leave Oxnard at 1 o'clock p.m.

One of the men on the ranch drove me to the station in time to catch this train. The single car was almost full of passengers. I suppose a lot of people, like myself, had been caught away from home and were anxious to get back.

A large number of the passengers left the train at Moorpark and some more at Simi. All those that were left got off at Santa Susana except a red headed German whiskey drummer and myself. We were the only two left.

The train just crawled along and stopped at the entrance to the Chatsworth tunnel. I got out to inquire what we were waiting for and was told that a man was going through the tunnel on foot to see if it was safe for the train, and we had to wait till he returned.

The train just crawled along into the tunnel and when it got to what seemed to be about the middle, it stopped and rocks began to fall on the roof. The red headed German whiskey drummer got panicky and said, "I have a gun, I will shoot myself, I will shoot myself." I said, "Don't be in a hurry, we may get out of here yet."

It's not a very pleasant feeling to think that the tunnel might cave in and bury us. After what seemed like a long time the train began to move again and slowly pulled out into the daylight.

The sunshine never was more welcome.

Two Tall Palms

In the summer of 1904 while Abbot Kinney was developing Venice, Dana Burke put in a subdivision on the adjoining property, known as Venice Annex. I think he wanted to do something spectacular to call attention to his project. Robert Armstrong, superintendent for the Abbot Kinney Company, suggested the planting of two or more tall palms which would be a sort of landmark. I was asked to supply the palms. I found two nice specimens of the Mexican Fan Palm (*Washingtonia robusta*) growing on a lot on South Hill Street, just north of 4th Street. A friend of mine happened to be the attorney for the lady who owned the property and through him I arranged to buy those two palms for $50.00. I quoted my customer a price of $500.00 for the two palms, moved and planted. I thought I was going to make some money out of this venture but I was in for a disappointment.

At that time I had a little Mexican fellow working for me named Pedro Estrada, everyone called him Pete. Well, Pete and I undertook the job of digging and boxing these two palms. We worked like gophers moving the soil. We dug the earth away, leaving a square of earth and roots 5 by 5 feet, around which we built a box of heavy redwood braced with iron rods. Those palms have quantities of roots about the size of a lead pencil and we had to keep chopping those with a hand axe as we proceeded with the work. It took us several days to dig and box the palms. Then we had a house mover named Mason come and load the boxes onto two low heavy trucks with a two wheeled trailer to carry the trunk. We went out Washington Boulevard one Sunday morning with six horses to each truck and it created quite a sensation.

Mason placed the palms in the holes which were already dug and braced each one with three guy wires.

After paying all expenses all I had left to pay for my time and Pete's was $40.00 and we really worked hard. However, it was a good experience. We measured the palms while they were laying down before loading onto the trucks. One measured 49 feet and the other 51 feet. The last time I saw these palms they had grown considerably and were about 70 feet tall.

Gathering Grevillea Seed

When I started in business in 1903 there was a good demand for seed of *Grevillea robusta*, both in the Eastern states and in Europe. Young plants of this Australian tree were grown by the thousands and sold as potted plants for house decoration. They were very popular in London's Covent Garden Market and were known by the common name of "Fern Trees." I received orders for quantities of the seed from firms in this country and in Europe.

The seed usually ripens in August and September and is collected by spreading a canvas sheet under the tree and shaking the branches, either by climbing the tree or with the aid of a long pole. It should be gathered early in the morning before the breeze comes up as the seed is very light and blows away easily. Also it must be a warm sunny morning. In damp or foggy weather the seed vessels close up tight and the seed will not drop out.

In 1904 I located a row of trees in Hollywood, loaded with seed. I went out there early one morning with a canvas sheet. I did not need a pole as the trees were small and I could easily climb them. It was a nice warm morning and the seed dropped freely. I worked fast in order to get through before the breeze came up. In a few hours I had nearly 20 pounds of seed. This was the best haul I ever made.

Remembering that Grevillea trees were planted on either side of Euclid Avenue from Ontario through Upland to San Antonio Heights, a distance of several miles, it occurred to me that this should be a good place to collect seed.

At that time I had working for me a man named P. H. Field who owned a horse and light wagon. We loaded some canvas sheets, a long pole, and some other paraphernalia onto his wagon and started him out early one morning. I went on the train and met him at Ontario late in the afternoon. We decided to start our work at the upper end of the Avenue, so drove on to San Antonio Heights. We found a beautiful orange grove and Field suggested that we camp here for the night so we obtained permission from the owner who lived nearby. We went to a little store and purchased some provisions for our supper and breakfast, I said to the store keeper, "Do you get any fog up here?" "Oh, no," he replied, "We never have any fog, that is the reason I live here," patting his chest with his hand. "Well," I said, "That's good news for us because we are here to gather seed off these Grevillea trees and we can't do anything on a foggy morning."

We cooked our supper and enjoyed it immensely. We walked around the neighborhood for awhile, then retired for the night in the orange grove. We spread one heavy canvas on the ground and used another one to cover us. I slept well but woke up about 4 o'clock and thought I could smell fog. When we got up after daylight the fog was so thick we could not see a tree across the street.

We had a good breakfast then waited around for the fog to clear away; after awhile the sun began to shine and we spread a canvas under a tree and shook the branches with our pole but nothing came down. By the time the sun had opened up the little seed vessels it was about 11 o'clock.

We spread our canvas under a tree and shook the branches down came the seed, but by this time the breeze had come up and took it clear over to the other side of the canvas sheet. The next time we placed our sheet a distance from the tree to allow for the wind, then just as we shook the branches there was a lull in the breeze and the seed came straight down onto the ground.

It was very aggravating. We did not get any seed but enjoyed camping in the orange grove.

Incidentally, I said, "Field, don't you wish you owned this beautiful orange grove?" He replied, "No, I don't. If I owned it I would have to care for the trees, spray them, irrigate them, pick the fruit, pay taxes and a whole lot of other things. Now I have had all the pleasure possible, I have slept among the trees, eaten the fruit, enjoyed the fragrance of the blossoms and I have nothing to worry about." Field was quite a philosopher, but I have already mentioned him in a previous story.

We gathered Grevillea seed in various places over a number of years. Small trees were the most satisfactory but as the time went by these became scarce as this tree had gone out of favor and no young trees were planted. We found a very good source for the seed at Corona and made trips there for several years. Then we returned to the trees on Euclid Avenue at Ontario but these trees had become so tall it was difficult to gather the seed. Only the lower branches could be reached even with a long pole and the best crop was usually at the top of the tree.

We then tried sweeping the seed up on the paved streets. My propagator, Oswald Hogland, would take the truck and one man and sometimes I would go in my car. We would sweep the street along by the curb for a distance of a mile or so, then sack up the sweepings and haul it to the nursery. After we got it home Oswald would spend several days running the sweepings through the seed cleaner to get out the leaves, sticks, dust, cigarette butts and other rubbish from the street. After the seed was finally cleaned it was all right, but the cost of the long trips and the time spent separating it from the rubbish was more than the seed was worth so I decided not to bother with it any more.

HOMER LEA

In September of 1907 I arranged to spend my vacation at Seven Oaks, a resort located in the Santa Ana Canyon of the San Bernardino Mountains. At that time there was no road there by way of the canyon so the camp was reached by taking a stage for fifteen miles from Redlands to Skinner's Ranch and then a ten mile horseback ride over a trail to the camp.

I arrived in camp late one afternoon and after dinner I went into the large room where the guests generally congregated of an evening. There, sitting by the fire, was a little hunchback fellow smoking an enormous pipe which looked all out of proportion to himself.

I thought, "What a strange looking little fellow." Just then a gentleman came up and introduced himself to me and said, "I am Wilfred Norman. I know you are well acquainted with my father and my brother Alfred." Then he said, "Mr. Payne, this is my wife, Mrs. Norman." We talked for awhile, then Mrs. Norman said, "Mr. Payne, I would like to introduce you to General Homer Lea," addressing the little fellow sitting by the fire. He rose and greeted me with a warm smile. I thought to myself, "What kind of a joke is this? A general! How could this deformed little fellow be a general?" Later Mrs. Norman explained it to me. She said, "Homer Lea is a military genius. There was, of course, no place for him in the armed forces of the United States, but in China it was different. There they were glad to avail themselves of his fertile brain. He is a great friend and supporter of Sun Yat-Sen of the revolutionary party." (Later Sun Yat-Sen became the first president of the Chinese Republic after the fall of the old dynasty). I was to see a good deal more of this little fellow during the next two weeks.

The next day I found out that Homer Lea had a little burro which he rode all over the mountains. This was no ordinary burro which are generally very slow. This burro would gallop along just like a horse. In fact, it could keep up with any of the saddle horses at the camp.

Homer Lea and I went on several trips together, sometimes it would be a half day trip, sometimes we would take our lunch and be gone all day. He knew all the canyons and trails in these mountains. He had spent nearly seven months exploring the San Bernardino, San Jacinto, San Gabriel and Tehachapi mountains from a military viewpoint, the results of which he later recorded in a book.

On one occasion, a whole group from the camp rode over the trail to Bear Valley, from there we went to Bluff Lake. Here Homer Lea left the party and went off by himself. A young man who owned a general store in Redlands undertook to guide the party back to Seven Oaks but after a little confessed that he did not know the way. Then Mrs. Crafts of Crafton, riding a white horse, said she knew a short cut down into the Santa Ana Canyon so we let her lead the party. I never descended a mountain so fast in my life. We had to lead our horses a good part of the time and we just slid down the mountain. If you stopped your horse would push you along so you had to keep going. When we reached the canyon it was easy and we soon came to the camp. When we got there Homer Lea had been home for two hours.

Homer Lea was a Los Angeles boy, went to high school here and later graduated from Stanford University. He had a brilliant mind and I never knew a man so well informed on all subjects. Many nights in camp we sat by the fire and talked and I never got tired of his company.

Mr. and Mrs. Norman were operating a boarding house in the old Banning residence situated on the hill over the Hill Street tunnel and Homer Lea, upon returning to Los Angeles, went to board there. I was married in late December and as our house would not be available for a month we took a room at Mrs. Norman's. I sat opposite Homer Lea at the dinner table each evening. He was always the life of the party. When he talked everyone listened. He had the most winning smile and charming manner which made up for his deformity and diminutive size. He wrote two books, one, "The Vermilion Pencil," a Chinese story, in 1908. The other, "The Valor of Ignorance" published in 1909, a military work which created quite a sensation.

He died here a few years later.

SEED COLLECTING AT REDONDO BEACH

One afternoon my wife and I went to Redondo Beach. We walked out onto the sand dunes where I usually collected seed of Bush Sunflower, White Snapdragon and a few other things. I found the Beach Wallflower was ripe, so while I gathered some of the seed, my wife sat down and read a magazine.

Pretty soon a woman came along and said to Mrs. Payne, "What's that man doing?" "Oh, he's a botanist," replied my wife. "A what?" the woman asked. "A botanist" Mrs. Payne repeated. "That's a man who studies plants." "Oh," said the woman. Then she came over to where I was. "What kind you get?" she said. "Does it make good tea?" "What's it good for, rheumatics?" "No," I replied. "I am collecting the seed to plant for the flowers."

"Makes a good tea, eh?" she exclaimed and started furiously to grab all she could. If she saw a plant before I did, she would try to beat me to it. I was only interested in the seed spikes but she took the whole plant. After gathering all she could carry in her apron she left.

I hope it cured her rheumatics.

A Carload of
Eucalyptus Trees

During the Eucalyptus boom in Southern California which started in 1907 and continued for five years, there was a good demand for young eucalyptus trees in flats. Quite a number of small Eucalyptus Nurseries sprang up almost overnight. Many of these were operated by people who had regular jobs and who did this work in their spare time. A man would rent a vacant lot, have a water meter installed, purchase a quantity of flats and seed and raise perhaps 50,000 or 100,000 trees.

I supplied many of these dealers with the seed and helped dispose of their young plants. My seed store at 345 S. Main Street soon became a sort of clearing house for eucalyptus seed and plants.

On one occasion I had a customer for a carload of young trees of the Red Gum (*Eucalyptus rostrata*) to be shipped to the San Joaquin Valley. I made arrangements to buy these trees from a man who raised them on a lot on Crocker Street. He was a stock broker by profession and had taken up eucalyptus raising as a side line.

I ordered a freight car, bought some lumber and hired a carpenter to load the car. This man had loaded several cars before and knew just how to do it. A layer of flats were placed on the floor and a frame work built up to accommodate another layer, then another and so on.

I think there were seven or eight of these layers and a car thus packed would hold about 60,000 trees. If I remember rightly, we put 58,000 in this particular car.

I had working for me at that time a young Mexican named Pedro Estrada, whom we all called Pete. Well, Pete and I undertook to load the flats onto trucks which took them down to the freight car. Under the flats were a lot of slugs and every time we picked up a flat we would get our hands and clothes covered with slime. It was the dirtiest job I ever had. We had a time getting our hands clean afterwards and had to burn our clothes. It was hard work too. When two of you have loaded 530 flats onto trucks you feel you have done something. But we were young then and did not mind the work. The man who bought the eucalyptus was to pay for them before the car left. He came into my store between 5 and 6 o'clock and brought the whole amount in cash. The sale price was $9.00 per 1,000 which made a total of $522.00, which he handed me in green backs.

I never had very much money in those days and did not have a safe in the store. What to do with $522.00 was a question. Of course, I could hide it in a sack of seeds but what if the building burned down. I finally decided to take it home with me. I wrapped up the green backs in a brown paper package and put it inside my coat pocket. At home I put it under my mattress.

The next morning, Mrs. Payne saw me take the package from under my mattress. She wanted to know what it was. I said, "It's the money I got for the carload of Eucalyptus trees." "How much is it?" she asked. "Five hundred and twenty-two dollars." I replied. "Oh" she said, "If I had known that I never would have slept a wink." "That's why I did not tell you," I said. At 10 o'clock I put the money in the bank, then gave the man who raised the trees a check for his portion of the deal. My commission was two dollars per 1,000, making a total of $116.00 and I really felt that I had earned it.

THE JUDGE'S SPITTOON

It happened a long time ago, I think it must have been between 1908 and 1910, though I am not sure. A young man asked me if I would appear as a witness for him in a court case involving the purchase of some apple trees. He was a customer of mine, a nice sort of a chap with red hair, blue eyes and a freckled face, but for the life of me I can't remember his name. I think he was somewhat of a tender foot or he would not have been caught in a deal like this.

It seemed he had entered into an agreement to purchase 2500 apple trees at $25.00 per hundred or a total of $625.00. He had paid $100.00 down, leaving a balance of $525.00 due. Then he found he had been stung and he was willing to forfeit his down payment and back out of the deal. The plaintiff, however, did not see it that way, he wanted to dispose of the trees and he wanted the $525.00, so he brought suit for fulfillment of contract. The trial was held in a small court room in an old building somewhere near Temple Street. The judge was an out of town judge, I think he came from San Bernardino but am not sure. All the furniture on the platform consisted of one small table about two feet square and a single straight-backed chair for the judge to sit on and a spittoon. His honor wore an ordinary business suit, a little on the seedy side and chewed tobacco.

When I was called to the witness stand the attorney for the prosecution challenged my qualifications as a witness but I had no difficulty in establishing the fact that I had been trained in the nursery business and that I now owned and operated a nursery and seed business of my own so consequently was familiar with the prices of trees. I stated that the present wholesale price of apple trees was $12.00 per hundred. Here the plaintiff interrupted and said, "But Mr. Payne, you don't understand, these trees are three years old." "Then" I said, "They are not worth anything. It is a well known fact among nurserymen that two year old apple trees sell for less than one year old trees. Here is a copy of the wholesale catalogue for this season of the Fancher Creek Nurseries of Fresno. One year old apple trees are priced at $12.00 per 100, two year old trees at $10.00 per 100. Here is a catalogue from the Davis County Nursery listing two year old apple trees at $8.00 per 100. Three year old trees are worthless."

I was followed on the stand by Mr. Ray R. Bishop, Agricultural Commissioner for Orange County. As the trees in question were in Anaheim, they came under his jurisdiction. He testified that the trees were badly infested with two pests, I have forgotten just what but think it was red scale and woolly aphis but am not sure. He would not allow the trees to be moved.

When the judge reviewed the case he paced up and down the platform, all the time chewing tobacco and occasionally stopping to use the spittoon. He said the evidence clearly showed the trees were not worth the money charged for them. At the same time, the defendant had entered into a contract and had then sought to back out, so was a welcher and the court had no use for a welcher. The court would not render a decision at this time but would take the case under advisement and would bring in a verdict at a later date.

Later I heard that the judge had ruled in favor of the defendant and had ordered the $100.00 deposit money returned, which seemed to me the only fair thing to do.

These apple trees were owned by a doctor. I don't know but it seems to me quite possible that he obtained them with some real estate and had been led to believe that they had some real value.

No one familiar with the nursery business would have spent money to care for trees unsold after the second year.

THE OMBU TREE

One day, a long time ago, probably about 1910, though I am not sure, my friend, West Cove, who came out from England with me and who lived in Hollywood, came into my store on South Main Street. We went out into the Nursery Sales yard at the back of the store for something he wanted. While there, I said, "Have you a place for a shade tree that grows real fast?" He said, "Yes, I think I have just the place for it." I then handed him a small plant about five inches high in a three inch pot. He looked at it rather contemptuously and said, "That little thing? Why, that will never make a tree." I said, "Don't you worry, it will grow faster than anything you have ever seen." He took it home to his place on Yucca Street in Hollywood and planted it in the corner at the back end of the lot, about ten feet from the boundary line. In seven or eight years it had grown into a large spreading tree with a trunk two feet in diameter and buttresses all around the base, some of them a foot high or more. This is the Ombu Tree of the Argentine, also called "La Bella Sombra", the tree of the beautiful shadow. The botanical name is *Phytolaca dioica* and it is related to the pokeweed or pokeberry, a perennial herb of the eastern states.

The Ombu has become a popular shade tree in Spain but has not been planted extensively in California though there are trees of it scattered around here and there. One large tree in Santa Barbara had a trunk eight feet in diameter and had to be removed on account of breaking up the street.

There were several large specimens on the Arthur Letta estate in Hollywood but these too were destroyed when the property was subdivided.

I did not see the tree on the West Cove place on Yucca Street again until many years later after they had moved away. One day I happened to be in that part of the neighborhood so thought I would go and look at this tree. I asked the lady who lived in the house if I might go back and look at the big tree in the back yard. I said, "You know, I raised that tree from seed." She could hardly believe it. It now had a trunk with a diameter of over four feet and the buttresses some of them two feet high had completely filled up the corner of the property.

She introduced me to the man next door and told him about this tree and he was greatly interested. "But," he said, turning and pointing to a Carob tree, "You didn't raise this one, no, this was planted here by the padres." I said, "I am sorry to disillusion you, my good friend, but that tree was planted by John Rapp. He used to own this property. John Rapp was quite a horticulturist and when he decided to subdivide this area he planted out a number of Carob and Red-flowering Eucalyptus trees. That was soon after I started in business in 1903, probably in the early part of 1904 or 1905."

I felt rather sorry afterwards that I had told this man the history of his tree for I think he received a lot of pleasure from his belief that the good old padres had actually planted it.

"Where ignorance is bliss, it is folly to be wise."

Navarro de Andrade

One day in the spring of 1910 a young man came into my store on South Main Street and handed me his card which read: Edmundo Navarro de Andrade, Forester—Paulista Railroad Company, São Paulo, Brazil. He said he had come to California to study eucalyptus culture here and had been referred to me as an authority on this subject. I told him I would be glad to help him in any way I could. It seems that after graduating from the College of Agriculture at Coimbra, Portugal, in 1903, he had returned to his native country of Brazil and had been engaged by the Paulista Railroad Company to establish a department of forestry for the company. The problem was to provide firewood for the trains and poles and ties for the railroad, also fence posts, because in Brazil the railroads have to be enclosed. He had experimented with some native trees and eucalyptus and finally decided on the latter on account of it's rapid growth.

The next day we went to the University of California Forestry Station in Santa Monica Canyon where there were about 80 species of eucalyptus planted. I introduced him to Norman Ingham who was in charge. We spent a few hours there and took some photographs.

The Eucalyptus boom was then at it's height and there were a number of eucalyptus nuseries scattered around the country. We visited the one at Inglewood owned by the Eucalyptus Timber Corporation where a million trees were being raised. Then we went to see the Rosecrans grove and a number of other places where eucalyptus were grown for firewood.

One day we took the Pacific Electric car to Cypress in Orange County where I had several men engaged in gathering a large quantity of *Eucalyptus tereticornis* seed. Later some of this seed went to Brazil.

Navarro de Andrade then took a trip to Santa Barbara to meet Ellwood Cooper and visit the Ellwood Ranch where a number of species of eucalyptus were growing. Ellwood Cooper was one of the early authorities on eucalyptus in California and commenced planting the trees on a large scale about 1870. In 1875 he gave a public address on eucalyptus which was later published in book form.

I helped Navarro de Andrade map out other trips to take together with the names of people he should meet. Every few days he would come into the store and tell me where he had been and what he had seen. Sometimes he would ask if I could show him a tree of a certain species, like *E. diversicolor* or *E. pilularis*, and usually I knew where one was to be seen not too far away. We measured trees and he took photographs.

After a few weeks here in which he gathered an amount of information from different sources he decided to go north. I was planning a trip north myself so arranged to meet him in San Francisco. We went to see the Sutro Grove where there were some large specimens of the common Blue Gum.

One day we went to San Jose to visit the Gillespie Saw Mill where eucalyptus lumber was handled in large quantities. After I left, Navarro de Andrade spent some time at Golden Gate Park and the University of California at Berkeley, also nurseries and commercial groves, interviewing different people and taking photographs. He then returned to Southern California and prepared to return to Brazil. He had spent about five weeks in California and had assembled a wealth of information. Soon after he left I sent him a large shipment of seed, and afterwards, two more, one and two years later.

In 1911 he published a book on 'Eucalyptus Culture In California'. This book is written in Portuguese but is filled with names of people and places familiar to me and is also profusely illustrated with photographs so I can get a very good idea of what it is about. I don't believe that anyone here has ever covered the subject of eucalyptus in California as completely as Navarro de Andrade did in this book.

In 1918 Navarro de Andrade again visited California. He was now married and brought his wife with him. He said, "Of course, you know Brazil is a great coffee producing country but we have to import all our sacks, so the government is sending me on a trip to investigate the jute industry. We want to grow the material and make our own sacks. We will visit most of the countries where jute is produced."

They were only here a few days but did have time to come out to the house for dinner one evening. My wife was quite nervous at the thought of making coffee for Brazilians. However, they said it was very good coffee but of course they had to be polite. I told them I had read a story in a magazine about Brazil in which it said, "If you asked a Brazilian how he liked his coffee he would reply, 'as black as night, as hot as hell and sweet as a woman's love'." I asked Navarro if that were true and he said, "Well, I don't know about that, but most of us do like it black and good and hot."

We had a very pleasant evening. Of course, we conversed further about eucalyptus. He had just published another book on the subject and presented me with an autographed copy. He said that he had now 5,000,000 trees growing and had land ready for 30,000,000 more. I asked him what the climate was like and he said very similar to that of Southern California except that the average rainfall is forty one inches. Then I asked him about the land and he said they had good rich valley lands. Finally I asked him what the cost of such land was and he said, "Five dollars per acre." I said, "No wonder you can make a success of growing eucalyptus trees." He said, "The primary purpose for growing these trees is to produce firewood, poles, ties and fence posts. Coal, in Brazil, is scarce and of poor quality so we use wood for fuel. We also produce charcoal, eucalyptus oil and a boiler compound."

Then the conversation changed to other matters. We talked about Brazil, about the people and their ways and customs. About the different countries they would visit and so on. After a very enjoyable evening I drove them back to their hotel.

Mr. and Mrs. Navarro de Andrade were only here in Los Angeles a few days then left on their trip and we did not see them again.

In the *Journal of Heredity* for July 1941, published by the American Genetic Association is an account of the presentation of the Meyer Medal to Dr. Edmundo Navarro de Andrade for his work with eucalyptus in Brazil. Following this presentation, a banquet was held at the Cosmos Club in Washington in his honor after which he gave a public address describing his work with eucalyptus in Brazil. During this address he stated that after his company had demonstrated the value of eucalyptus other companies had become interested in planting these trees and there were now growing in Brazil over 100,000,000 eucalyptus trees.

GATHERING EUCALYPTUS SEED

During the Eucalyptus boom in California which started in 1907 and lasted for about five years, there was a great demand for eucalyptus seed, especially *Eucalyptus rostrata* and *Eucalyptus tereticornis*. If I remember correctly, I had one contract for 300 pounds of *Eucalyptus rostrata* and 200 pounds of *Eucalyptus tereticornis* and another order for 200 pounds of each, besides a great many smaller orders.

We had no trouble in collecting the *Eucalyptus rostrata* as there were many trees of this species scattered around the country. But *Eucalyptus tereticornis* was different. We would find a tree here and there and obtain a pound or so of seed, but this was nothing compared to the orders we must fill. Frankly, I did not know what to do.

Then one day, a man came into my store on Main Street with a sample of eucalyptus seed and asked me what it was. I said, "That is *Eucalyptus tereticornis*." I was just about to ask him where he found it when he volunteered the information. He said, "If you want any seed, I can tell you where there is plenty of it. You take the Pacific Electric car that runs to Santa Ana and get off at Cypress, then walk east a short distance and you will see a whole row of these trees."

So, on Sunday morning, I took the Pacific Electric car to Cypress, then walked east as the man had said, and sure enough, here was a whole row of these trees just loaded with seed. Upon inquiry I found the trees belonged to George B. Miller, a rancher who owned the adjoining property. I went to his house and found him home. I told him I would like to get some seed off these trees.

He said, "Just help yourself," thinking, of course, that I wanted a small quantity. I said, "Mr. Miller, you don't understand, I don't want you to give me the seed, I expect to pay for it and I want a large quantity." He then asked how the seed was gathered. I explained to him that we cut off the branches bearing the seed vessels and spread them out on a canvas sheet. In a few days the valves of the seed vessels open up and the seed drops out on the canvas. He did not like the idea of having the trees trimmed and it looked as though I was not going to be able to make a deal.

It so happened that the United States government had commissioned me to procure six boles of this species of eucalyptus for a piling test in San Francisco Bay. I said, "Mr. Miller, the United States government has commissioned me to secure six trees of this kind for a piling test and I have not been able to find them any where till now. You have exactly what is wanted and I can pay you $20.00 apiece for six trees." "Well!" he said, "If the government wants them it looks as though I should let you have them." Before I left I made arrangements to buy six of these trees. A few days later I took two men down there and we selected six trees that came up to the government specifications and also that had plenty of seed. We cut them down and loaded the six boles on a flat car and shipped them to San Francisco. We collected a nice amount of seed but not nearly enough. I told my foreman, P. J. Wheldon, if he had a chance to talk to Mr. Miller, to see if we could buy the whole row of trees. He telephoned me later in the day that he had talked with Miller and he seemed to be in a good mood and would take $500.00 for the whole row of trees. I told Wheldon to write out a contract and to give Miller a check for $100.00 on account, the balance to be paid before we cut the trees. This Wheldon did, and Miller signed it. The next day, to my great surprise, here comes George Miller into my store on Main Street and wants to back out of the deal. It seems that after he had made the deal the day before, his wife came home and gave him the devil. I said, "Mr. Miller, you signed an agreement and accepted a payment of $100.00 on account. I don't think it would be very honorable for you to back out now. Besides, if you hired a man to chop these trees down and cut them up into firewood, and had $200.00 left after paying the labor bill, you would be lucky. Now I have given you $120.00 and am giving you $500.00 more, making a total of $620.00, and you don't have to do a thing. I can't think of any way you could make $620.00 as easily as that and I don't believe you want to pass it up. The eucalyptus sprout from the stump and in a few years you will have a row of trees again."

He seemed pacified and went home feeling that he was fortunate in making such a good deal.

I bought canvas sheets; took Wheldon and another man from Los Angeles down to Cypress; hired two more men from the neighborhood and went to work cutting the trees and gathering the seed. We had canvas sheets spread out on the ground in every direction. Altogether we collected nearly 1200 pounds of seed. We filled our orders and new ones that kept coming. We sold a great deal of seed locally and also shipped quantities to Arizona, Texas, Florida, Cuba, Isle of Pines, Brazil and other countries. The price was $8.00 per pound.

The Eucalyptus boom burst about 1912. There was now no demand for seed or trees. I had over a hundred pounds of seed on hand. Nobody wanted it.

Two Little Bugs

In 1912 I shipped five carloads of citrus trees to customers in Ventura County. The next year I received an order for one carload of orange trees from Mr. Leonard, one of my former customers. This order was conditional upon my being able to deliver the trees in Ventura County. Mr. Leonard said he understood the regulations on citrus trees coming into the county were much more strict than in previous seasons, so I wrote to Mr. R. Vail, the Agricultural Commissioner for Ventura County, whose office was in Santa Paula and asked him if citrus trees would be allowed to come into the county. I told him the trees would come from Villa Park in Orange County, grown by Dr. Poppelwell, the same grower and the same place as the trees shipped the year before. Vail replied that citrus stock could come into Ventura County provided the trees were clean and were given the following treatment. Trees must be defoliated, dipped in rosin wash and fumigated. I then wrote and asked Vail if he would like to send a representative to supervise this treatment or whether it would be satisfactory if Mr. Ray R. Bishop, the commissioner for Orange County, supervised the work. He replied that it would be perfectly satisfactory to have Bishop look after it.

In the course of time the trees were treated as per specifications, loaded and the car sent on it's way. A couple of days later I received a telegram from Vail which said, "Carload of citrus trees here consigned by you badly infested with live red scale, cannot remain in Ventura County. Must be returned immediately or will be destroyed." I could not understand this for I knew Dr. Poppelwell had followed Vail's instructions in treating the trees and Mr. Bishop had certified them as clean. I telephoned to Vail and asked him what could be done. He said the trees could be fumigated so I told him to have this done and send me the bill. I thought this would settle the matter but the next morning Vail phoned me that the car of citrus trees had been fumigated and was still infested with live red scale and could not remain in Ventura county but would have to be returned or destroyed. I told him I would come to Oxnard in the morning. He said, "It won't do you any good, the trees will have to be destroyed." I said, "Well, I am going to come anyway. Just hold everything till I get there. That car contains 1,000 orange trees the price of which is $1.00 each or $1,000 for the carload. You can't destroy that property without further investigation."

I phoned to Dr. Poppelwell at Villa Park and told him what had happened. He said he would come into Los Angeles in the afternoon and go with me next day. Later in the day Dr. Poppelwell walked into my store on South Main Street and I was greatly relieved to see Ray Bishop with him. Now it would be one county commissioner against another. We met next morning by appointment at the Arcade Depot and took the 8 o'clock train for Oxnard. We hired a car and chauffeur to drive us to the Edfu siding where the car of citrus trees had been switched. Before leaving we phoned to Vail to meet us there. We got there first and had to wait nearly half an hour for Vail. He and Bishop engaged in a conversation for about twenty minutes. Then they both got up into the car of orange trees to look for red scale. They could not find any, then after awhile they found two. They both agreed that one was dead but could not agree about the other one. They were the only red scale they found. Still Vail was very stubborn. He would not consent to the trees staying in the county. He and Bishop argued all morning and had not reached any agreement by lunch time. We had lunch at Mr. Leonard's house and arguments were suspended during the meal but were well resumed afterwards. At one time Bishop got a little out of patience and said, "Vail, you have red scale in Ventura County and you know it. I bet I could find some in less than two hours." Vail did not contradict this statement. Dr. Poppelwell and I both joined in occasionally but we left most of the debate to the two commissioners.

They talked for at least an hour and a half more. Then Vail finally said, "If you will fumigate the car, then take the trees out and scrub each one with rosin wash, we will reinspect them. We do not promise to pass the trees but that is all we can do." Dr. Poppelwell and I agreed to this. We drove to Ventura and went to the Shepherd Nursery and borrowed some fumigating pots, then we got the sulfuric acid and cyanide and went to the car of citrus trees. Dr. Poppelwell put the acid in the pots and placed them among the trees, then dropped in the cyanide and quickly got out of the car. Then he tried to shut the door but it would not move. He said to me, "This door is stuck, help me with it." We both pushed on the door but it would not budge. We then called the chauffeur to help us and all three pushed but could not move it. Then Dr. Poppelwell looked at it more closely and said, "Why, it is nailed, just the way I nailed it at Orange before the car left. I nailed it open a few feet so the trees would have some ventilation in transit." I looked at Dr. Poppelwell and said, "Then if Vail's men fumigated the car, as claimed, they did it with the door open."

Vail never sent me a bill for that fumigation so I let it pass. Dr. Poppelwell stayed over and hired a man to help him the next day take the trees out and scrub them with rosin wash. This time, Vail finally released the shipment and Mr. Leonard was able to proceed with planting his grove of orange trees.

There was no stock of young orange trees available in Ventura County at that time, and had this stock been refused entry to the county Mr. Leonard would have had to defer his planting for two or three years, all on account of two little bugs.

The Train Was Late

In the spring of 1914 John Ruopp, an old friend of mine and superintendent of the Patterson Ranch at Oxnard, engaged me to do some landscaping on the Tapo Ranch which was also under his management. The Tapo Ranch is located a few miles from Santa Susanna and I arranged to go there on a Sunday morning. One of my men, P. H. Field, accompanied me and we took the early morning train from the Arcade Depot at Fifth Street, near Central Avenue. Arriving at Santa Susanna we were met by a man who drove us to the ranch. We looked over the area to be landscaped, measured it, and made a rough drawing and some notes to take home with us.

In the afternoon we had some spare time so went for a walk up one of the canyons. We saw some tall bushes in bloom and I could not imagine what they could be. Then, when we got a little nearer, I was surprised to find that they were giant lupines. I had never seen anything like them before. Many of the bushes were seven or eight feet tall and covered with long racemes of fragrant flowers. The colors varied from lavender to various shades of blue, purple, pink, orchid and one white. No two seemed to be just alike.

I returned to this spot a few years later and collected specimens of this plant for Dr. Anstruther Davidson, the veteran botanist of Los Angeles, who named it *Lupinus paynei* and published it's description in the *Bulletin of the Southern California Academy of Sciences* for July, 1918.

The train for Los Angeles was due to leave Santa Susanna soon after 5 o'clock and we were driven to the depot. Soon, a whole band of musicians arrived from the Ettie Maier Ranch. It seems there had been a big party there. These musicians had come from Los Angeles to furnish the music and were now returning home. So there was quite a crowd waiting for the train. Two others came along a few minutes later. They were two young fellows who had been chopping wood for a few months in the mountains and wanted to go to the city for a few days.

The train was late, 6 o'clock, then seven, then eight. At 8 o'clock the Station Master turned us all out of the building as he said he closed up at that time and he wanted to retire.

This made us all very angry, a condition that was not improved by the fact that we had had no supper and there was no place where any could be procured. The drummer beat his drum and the band began to play. They marched round and round the building singing Salvation Army hymns and other songs. If the Station Master wanted to retire he could but he was not going to get any sleep.

Nine o'clock came and no train. The two wood choppers rustled up some pieces of wood and made a fire. We all sat around the fire and talked and once in awhile we had a little music or a song. One fat man persuaded one of the girls to sit on his lap. Then he said, "Oh, if my wife could see me now." and again, "Oh, if my wife could see me now." One of the others said to me, "You know, he has no wife so he is perfectly safe."

Ten o'clock came and still no train. The two wood choppers rustled up some more wood to keep the fire going. Eleven o'clock came—still no train. It bogan to look as though we were going to be here all night and it was getting real cold. The wood choppers pulled down an old fence, posts and all to keep our fire burning. We were all getting very tired and some of us lay on the ground and dozed off for a few minutes.

It was nearly 1 o'clock when the train finally came along. When we got to Los Angeles, all the street cars had stopped running. I was then living on Manzanita Street, near Sunset Boulevard, so had to take a taxi cab. It was about 3 o'clock when I got home.

I thought my wife would be terribly worried but she was not. When I did not come home, she concluded I had had to stay over for some reason or other.

She said, "Why didn't you take a room down town? You know what a gossip our neighbor is. If she saw you come home in a taxi at 3 o'clock in the morning you know what she would make of it." I said, "It should make her real happy."

EUCALYPTUS IN LIBYA

Upon my first visit to Santa Barbara in 1896 I made the acquaintance of Dr. F. Franceschi who had established a nursery on the corner of State and Gutierrez Streets. He specialized in rare plants and in the years that followed I had occasion to meet him frequently.

After the war between Italy and Turkey in 1911 and 1912, Libya became Italian territory. The Italian government asked Dr. Franceschi to return to Italy and accept the position of Agricultural Commissioner for Libya with headquarters in Tripoli. After he moved there I corresponded with him. In one of his letters he said, "In this vast country nearly four times the size of California I have only found four eucalyptus trees planted here by the Turks. Will you please send me seed of as many kinds as you can so that I may try them in this new country?" I sent him 43 species, if I remember correctly.

About two years ago I received a letter from Dr. Franceschi's son who is living in Italy, requesting me to send some seeds to his sister, Ernestina, now carrying on her father's work at Tripoli.

In the same letter he wrote, "You will no doubt be interested to know that fully 90% of all the eucalyptus trees now growing in Tripolitania (about 7/8 of Libya) are the direct descendants of the seed you sent to my father back about 1914."

The Ants Go to Work

In 1919 I grew five acres of tomatoes for seed. It was a new variety which I put on the market the following year under the name of Payne's Victory. I had a splendid crop and made arrangements with a food supply company to use the fruit for tomato puree and give me back the seed. The company loaned me the lug boxes. We would make a picking and haul the tomatoes to the factory, then call the next day for the seed.

The last picking was made in October and we had the boxes setting out in the field all ready to take to the factory. Then that night it rained. It rained the next day and the next. By the time the weather cleared up, the tomatoes were rotting and it was useless to take them to the factory. So I had to devise some way to clean out the seed. I had a man in charge of my nursery at that time named Jesse Vore and he and I rigged up an apparatus for this purpose. First, we would dump a lug box of tomatoes into a round wash tub and mash them up thoroughly, then pour this into a wooden flume and with a series of screens and running water separate the seed from the skins and pulp. It worked like a charm but the tomatoes were rotting and full of white maggots. When these little fellows would touch the water they would curl up and were exactly the same size as the seed and went right on through with it. Jesse said, "How are we ever going to separate the maggots from the tomato seed?" I said, "Don't worry about that now, we'll find some way to get rid of them."

We took the seed to my nursery, which was on South Hoover Street at that time. There was an old greenhouse which was not in use just then. We put newspapers on the benches and spread the seed out to dry. It was a mass of white, wriggling little objects. The next morning I went into the greenhouse and I could hardly believe my eyes. I called out, "Jesse, come here. I'll show you how we are going to get rid of the maggots." An army of ants had moved in and were at work. Every ant carried a maggot. They worked all day and by nightfall scarcely a maggot was left.

I afterwards used this method with lupine seed. One of my men had collected seed of a Bush Lupine. That year many of the pods were badly infested with maggots. He brought the seed to me in a wire screen and said, "I have cleaned out the hulls, but I can't get rid of these white worms." I said, "I'll tell you what to do. Take the screen down to the field and set it on the ground by one of those red ant hills. Then go back in a few hours, and you'll find the worms have disappeared." It worked perfectly and we did this on several occasions. It won't do in all cases, however, as the ants are very fond of some kinds of seed. This is especially true of the Common Blue Gum. I have known of nurserymen having trouble with ants digging up the seed out of a seed bed.

I once had a Blue Gum blow down in my wild flower field and I had the brush cut and put on a canvas sheet so as to get the seed. In a few days the seed was shedding out and it looked as though I was going to have a nice lot. About a week later I went to throw the brush off the canvas and clean up the seed when I found it was all gone. I got down on my hands and knees; a few ants were still there just finishing up the job. They had taken every bit of it.

THE OTHER FELLOW'S SHOE

I have always been near sighted so have worn glasses most of my life. I wear them all the time except when I am asleep. On camping trips I invariably forget to take something along to put my glasses in at night, so I conceived the idea of using one of my shoes. The last thing I do before retiring is to take a shoe, put my glasses in it, then place the shoe near my pillow so I can reach for it first thing in the morning when I get up.

On one occasion, when travelling on a train at night, I was confronted with the same problem, what to do with my glasses? I decided to do the same as when camping in the mountains so I reached for a shoe, put my glasses in it then placed the shoe in the net provided for clothes. Of course, when the porter shined the shoes in the morning, I would have only one polished shoe. Perhaps he would conclude he had a one-legged men in this berth.

The next morning I got up, dressed, and put on my shoes and lo and behold! They were both beautifully polished. How could this be? It was a miracle. Then I happened to look in the lower berth I had occupied. Oh horrors! There in the net was the shoe I had used to store my glasses. Evidently I had taken some one else's shoe. It must belong to the man in the upper berth. There stood it's mate alone on the floor and beautifully polished.

I thought I should explain the matter to the owner but he showed no signs of getting up and I hated to awaken him. I went to breakfast and when I returned he had dressed and was gone. I looked around for a man with one unpolished shoe but did not see him.

I thought afterwards, if the passenger took the porter to task for not shining both his shoes, the porter could swear on a stack of Bibles that only one shoe was there. On the other hand the passenger could swear there were two and could point to the shoes to prove it.

Where that shoe had been, will to these two, forever be a mystery.

BABY QUAIL CROSSING A STREAM

In the spring of 1926, in the company of a young man named Douglas Black who was in my employ at that time, I made a seed collecting trip to the Colorado Desert. We collected seed of the Desert Sand Verbena and some other kinds at Thermal, then worked our way up the valley and stopped at Palm Springs on our way home.

We went up Palm Canyon. Douglas stopped to take some pictures as I went on a short distance by myself. As I rounded a turn in the canyon I came upon a scene I shall never forget. There was an old quail with one little one on the other side of the stream and four little ones on this side. The old bird was calling them and the little ones were crying as though their hearts would break. "You old fool!" I said, "How do you expect those tiny babies to get across that stream?" It was at least twelve feet wide and quite deep. I caught one little fellow and found a place where I could cross on some rocks and carried it across where it ran off to join it's mother. The old bird kept calling, all the time going further away and not taking the slightest notice of the little ones she had left behind on the other side of the stream. I tried to catch another one but it seemed to be frightened and all of a sudden flopped into the stream. "There," I said, "That's the end of you." But no! It wasn't. The little fellow floated like a leaf on the water and there was enough curve in the stream at this point so that the current took it to the other side, then it climbed up the bank and went off to join it's mother. Then the next one went across and then the last one went to join the rest.

I felt very cheap. Evidently the old bird knew this was a good spot to choose to cross the stream and was telling her babies not to be afraid to jump in and they would land safely on the other side. I said, "Dear Lady Quail, I offer you my humble apology. Mother knows best."

THE GAME KEEPER'S SON

One day, a long time ago, probably in the late twenties, a man came into my nursery and said, "I am a gardener looking for a job." From his accent I knew he was English, though I don't think he knew that I was. I said, "What part of the old country did you come from?" "Oh," he replied, "YOU wouldn't know it." I said, "How do you know I wouldn't know it?" "Well," he said, "It's a little village in Northamptonshire named Harleston." I said, "I certainly should know it for I was born and raised in Church Brampton, the very next village." The man was quite surprised. Then he said, "Do you remember Earl Spencer's gamekeeper?" "Yes," I said. "His name was Kirby, a tall man with a long blonde beard." "Well," he replied, "That man was my father."

I telephoned to George Hendry, my foreman on the Knight estate (the place I had charge of for so many years) in Santa Barbara and we gave Kirby a job to look after the greenhouse, lath house, cut flower garden etc. He turned out to be a very good gardener and just what we needed. A nice little house on the place went with the job so he and his wife were very comfortable there.

Speaking of Harleston, when I was a little boy on the farm we used to bake our own bread. In those days you could not go to the market to buy yeast, as now-a-days, but had to get it from a brewery where it was generally called "balm". The village of Harleston was the nearest place where we could procure it. So one day my Aunt Mary, who lived with us, asked my brother Frank to ride over to Harleston and get some balm. He rode a bay horse named David and took a can for the balm. On the way back he accidentally fell in with a bunch of fox hunters. Old David thoroughly enjoyed it and went right along with the other horses, clearing the hedges and ditches just as they did. My brother, however, was somewhat embarrassed when the hunters stared wonderingly at the tin can he carried which he had to admit was slightly out of place on a fox hunt.

A Trip to Santa Cruz Island

In September of 1928 the Nature Club of Southern California sponsored a three day trip to Santa Cruz Island. The club chartered a boat with Captain Eaton to take us from Santa Barbara to the island. We assembled on' the pier at Santa Barbara and parked our cars. There were about sixty of our members and around thirty others who joined the group in order to take advantage of the special rates. Among those who joined the excursion were Ralph Hoffman, Director of the Santa Barbara Natural History Museum, Robert Canterbury from the Blaksley Botanic Garden, Dr. Lovell from the *Los Angeles Times* and a number of doctors and other professional men. The total cost was to be prorated among the number taking the trip so the more that went the lower the rate. We boarded the boat at 10 o'clock. It was a beautiful day, the sun was shining, the sky was blue and the ocean calm and smooth. The trip was delightful and as we neared the island with it's rocky coastline it seemed as if we were about to enter an enchanted land.

We reached Pelican Bay and Eaton's camp in time for lunch. There is no beach here and we were taken ashore in row boats which landed us onto a wooden platform, then we climbed a lot of steps up to the camp. Our luggage was pulled up with a cable. The dining room was a long building looking out over the ocean. Cabins and tents were scattered around in different directions. Mrs. Payne and I had a cabin just a short distance from headquarters.

There were no roads and, of course, no automobiles. Trails led to different parts of the island. In the afternoon a few of us explored the canyon back of the camp. The most interesting thing we saw was the Ironwood trees, (*Lyonothamnus floribundus asplenifolius*). The canyon is quite steep and in the winter, after the rain water pours down over the bedrock, usually on each side of the water-course is a bench of rocky soil and this is where the Ironwoods grow. Often they are crowded thickly together and do not make the handsome specimens we are used to seeing in cultivation.

After the evening meal we had a short program put on by members of the club and a few others who were in the party. Then we retired for a peaceful night's rest away from all the noises of modern civilization.

On Sunday morning a large number of the club went for a four mile hike over a trail which went up and down through several canyons but finally brought us to a beach where there was a landing. A road, the only one on the island we were told, went a few miles up the canyon to a ranch house. A Ford truck, the only one on the island, was used on this ranch.

The most interesting plant seen on this trip was the Summer Holly, (*Comarostaphylis diversifolia*), the bushes of which were loaded with clusters of ripe red berries. Other noticeable plants were the island Lilac (*Ceanothus arboreus*), Island Oak (*Quercus tomentella*), Bishop Pine (*Pinus muricata*) and, of course, the island Buckwheat, (*Eriogonum arborescens*) which was very plentiful. Growing on a steep cliff was a very attractive gray leaved plant which Ralph Hoffman identified as *Hazardia cana*. While Ralph Hoffman's specialty was birds, he was a good all-around naturalist and we were fortunate to have his company on this trip.

Monday morning I spent some time collecting seed of the Summer Holly, Island Buckwheat and Hazardia, all I which had not collected or grown previously.

After lunch on Monday, (Labor Day), our party boarded the boat for the return trip to the mainland. The sea was quite rough and many of the passengers were seasick, including several doctors. The boat was crowded, a fact we did not mind when the weather was good and we could walk around. Now we lay on the deck like a bunch of sardines. Everybody was glad when we landed again at the pier in Santa Barbara. We had had a wonderful time except for the return trip. The total charge to each one was $12.85. This included transportation both ways, two night's lodging and seven meals, and the meals were good.

It was one of the most enjoyable trips I have ever had and certainly the least expensive.

THE STOLEN SYCAMORE SEED

One Sunday, along about 1928 or 1929, I was in Santa Monica Canyon, and, noticing that the sycamore seed was ripe, I commenced to gather it from some trees growing on a piece of vacant ground. There was one tree well loaded with seed, of which the branches came down low making it especially easy to gather. The tree itself stood in somebody's yard, but the branches came over the fence onto the vacant lot. I moved over and started to gather seed off this tree. In a few minutes a man came tearing out and yelling, "I caught you, I caught you stealing." "Why my good fellow," said I, "This seed is all falling on the ground and will be blown away in a few days. What can possibly be the objection to my picking some of it before it goes to waste?" I went on, "I have a nursery in which I raise native plants and all I want is a few handfuls of seed to plant to raise more sycamore trees. These trees will in time be planted out and help make the country more beautiful." Besides, I said, "Do you own this lot?" "No, I don't" he replied. "Well," I said, "I have not trespassed on your property and you have no jurisdiction over that portion of the tree on this side of the fence."

The man was blind with rage and would not listen to reason. He wanted to fight, then he was going to have me arrested. I said, "Go ahead and have me arrested if you want to, I haven't done anything wrong. I'll give you my name and address." He took my card, got out his car and chased off down to the police station.

I had luncheon with Mr. and Mrs. Hugh Evans in Santa Monica and told them of my experience. "Why," they said, "The fellow must be crazy!" "Well," I said, "I think I will stop at the police station and see if he really did turn in a complaint." So, on my way home, I called at the Santa Monica Police Station. "I came to give myself up." I told the officer, "I am accused of the crime of picking sycamore seed in the Santa Monica Canyon."

"Oh," said the officer, "That fellow was here madder than a hornet. He's nuts, just forget it."

I raised a beautiful lot of young trees from the "stolen sycamore seed."

THE CUFF OF THE PANTS

One day, some time ago, I think it must have been in the late twenties, a man came to my store on South Main Street and asked me if I would identify some seeds for him. He said Dr. Anstruther Davidson, the botanist, had referred him to me. I looked at the seeds, there were three kinds. One was the Australian Saltbush (*Atriplex semibaccata*), a plant from Australia, now naturalized here on waste ground. The second was the Hedge Mustard (*Sisymbrium officinale*), a common weed on vacant lots and originally from Europe. The third was the Small Leaved Privet used so much at that time for hedges and known in nurseries as *Ligustrum nepalense*, though there seems to be some doubt about the correctness of the specific name.

I wrote the names down and asked the man what it was all about. He said it was a case in court but I would not have to appear so I dismissed the matter and thought no more of it. However, a few months later I was called to appear in court. It was a murder case, a young fellow was accused of killing his father in a quarrel over some money. The three kinds of seeds were found in the cuff of his pants. There was a privet hedge in the garden of the house where the crime was committed and it was claimed the defendant went through this hedge and then ran across a vacant lot where the other two plants were growing.

I identified the seeds, gave the court the common and scientific names of the plants and told how the Australian Saltbush had been introduced in the early nineties by the Department of Agriculture as a forage plant but had now become naturalized on vacant land up and down the coast. I was only away from my business a few hours and it really did not cause me much inconvenience. However, the defense called me back and the attorney asked if the Australian Saltbush grew in Venice and I said, "Yes, it does." Then he asked if the Hedge Mustard grew there and I said, "Yes, that grows there too." "What about the Privet?" he asked. "Does that grow in Venice too?" I replied, "1 don't remember seeing a hedge of this plant there but it is so generally planted that it is more than likely it is there." I found out afterwards that the defendant claimed he was in Venice at the time the crime was committed.

The fellow was convicted but the case was appealed and he got a second trial. I was called again and it caused me considerable inconvenience because I had to appear at court several times before I was called to the witness stand. Leo Aggeler was the attorney for the prosecution and Paul Schenk attorney for the defense. I thus became acquainted with both these gentlemen. It was interesting to watch them in action. In court they seemed about to devour one another. At recess time they were perfectly friendly. They sat on the benches in the outer hall with the rest of us and talked, now it was Leo and Paul.

I think the seeds must have played a rather important part in this case for I afterwards heard that it became known in the annals of the court as the "Mustard Seed Case." How it came out I am not sure. I think the young fellow was found guilty but was sent to some institution. Paul Schenk became a good customer of mine. He came to the nursery on a number of occasions and purchased plants. He was a very interesting man and I always enjoyed talking with him.

PRESSED FLOWERS

One day, a long time ago, a man phoned me at my store on South Main Street and asked if I would identify some pressed flowers for him. I asked him how many there were and he said, "Not more than a half dozen." So I told him to bring them to the store and I would see what I could do. A little later he arrived with the flowers. If I remember right, there were four or five of them. One was a Mary Semple aster, another Agripina rose and the others I have now forgotten. However, they were all common garden flowers. He said, "Can you tell me if these flowers were grown in California and if these specimens are eighteen years old?" "That," I said, "No one could tell. They are all common garden flowers and might have been grown in any part of the world. As far as the age of these specimens go, that depends entirely on the way in which they have been kept. They are not new varieties and were all obtainable eighteen years ago. They may be eighteen years old, or thirty years or more."

I said, "What's this all about?" He said, "It's in the Lucky Baldwin estate case. A woman claims that Lucky Baldwin married her eighteen years ago and is the father of her seventeen year old daughter. She and Baldwin spent their honeymoon on the Baldwin Ranch and he picked these flowers there and gave them to her at that time." I said, "You haven't the slightest bit of evidence here. If the flowers had been California wild flowers that were indigenous to the Baldwin Ranch, you might have a point but these are common garden flowers and could have been grown in any part of the world."

I never heard any more of the case.

CHUPAROSA

The Andreas Canyon Club was founded by Dr. George P. Clements and a group of men who appreciated this spot and wished to see it preserved in all it's natural beauty. One rule of the club was that any buildings erected must be built of the native stone and must fit into the landscape. Another rule was that only native plants could be planted in the canyon.

I spent a very pleasant week end there as the guest of Dr. Clements and Harold J. (Buddy) Ryan. I am not sure whether it was in 1929 or 1930, anyway, Monday was Washington's birthday, so it gave us a three day holiday. I went in Buddy Ryan's car with Dr. Clements and his son in law, Cliff Argue, Dr. Herbert S. Adair and Joe Stace. Harry Carr of the Los Angeles Times, Charlie Owen, artist for the Times, and Ralph D. Cornell joined the party at the canyon coming in their own cars. This made nine in our party, a nice group of fellows, and we had a wonderful time. Dr. Clements did most of the cooking but we all took turns at washing dishes and other work.

Sunday morning we spent exploring the canyon, which is very narrow in some places and there is not much of a trail.

Of course, the outstanding feature is the beautiful Fan Palms, (*Washington filifera*). In one place there is a tall palm standing out by itself, much larger than any of the others. J. Smeaton Chase in some of his writings referred to this palm as "La Reina del Canyon."

I found a few specimens of the Desert Apricot, (*Prunus fremontii*) and quite a few of the Goat Nut or Jojoba (*Simmondsia californica*) and, of course, plenty of the Cat's Claw (*Acacia gregii*) with it's sharp prickles. On Monday morning some of the group went to the Salton Sea.

Mrs. King C. Gillette had a beautiful place near Palm Springs and had asked me many times to stop and see her. I thought this would be a good opportunity, so Ralph Cornell, Dr. Adair and I drove down in Ralph's car. Her home was between Andreas Canyon and Palm Springs so we did not have far to go. The maid who came to the door did her very best to prevent us from seeing Mrs. Gillette, I suppose it was part of her job. Finally I got out of patience and said, "Will you please take a message to Mrs. Gillette? Tell her Theodore Payne is here." The next minute Mrs. Gillette came out herself and welcomed us. She showed us her house and many of the treasures she had collected, for she was a lady who had traveled in many parts of the world.

After awhile we went out into the garden which was beautifully laid out and contained many plants from the deserts of California and Arizona, together with some exotics which thrive under desert conditions. There were several good specimens of the Chuparosa (*Beloperone californica*) in full bloom. I had seen some of these while in the car on the way to Andreas Canyon but this was the first opportunity I had had of seeing it at close range and I was much interested, it being the only member of the Acanthus family native to California.

I looked for some seeds but only found green capsules. I gathered a few of these and Mrs. Gillette said, "I don't think they will grow, Mr, Payne, they are too green." "Well," I said, "I can try them, I have found sometimes that seeds not quite ripe will germinate." As a matter of fact, nearly every seed grew and I have grown the plant ever since, sometimes from seed and sometimes from cuttings.

After spending some time in the garden we went back into the house and wrote our names in Mrs. Gillette's guest book. There, just two spaces ahead of us, was the name of Albert Einstein who had been there a few days before.

We had spent two very enjoyable hours in this beautiful place with a most charming hostess. After we left Dr. Adair said, "I wouldn't have missed this for the world but I thought for awhile we were not going to get in there. Your name seems to be a magic word." "It's not a magic word," I said, "But it so happens that I had a good deal to do with the planting of Mrs. Gillette's gardens, both in her former home at Santa Monica and also the one on the ranch near Calabasas. When she asked me to call and see her here I knew she meant it."

It was now nearly noon so we returned to Andreas Canyon and after lunch left for home, after a most enjoyable three days vacation.

The Tree He Planted

It is difficult to estimate the age of a tree by it's size. A tree may grow more the first ten years than during the next twenty years. I have known Blue Gums (*Eucalyptus globulus*) to grow sixty feet and more in five years. On the other hand some eucalyptus trees in front of my old nursery site at South Hoover and 33rd Streets don't look to be any bigger than when I started my nursery there in 1910, fifty years ago. These trees are planted in a rather narrow parkway with paved Hoover Street on one side and a side walk and parking lot on the other, so they don't have much of a chance.

Many years ago a botanist friend of mine, the late Fred E. Burlew, built a new home on Valley View Boulevard in Glendale. His lot was 100 x 300 feet so he had plenty of room for trees. He purchased a number of plants from me and asked me many times to come and see his place. Somehow or other I never seemed to get around to do so. Then one day, I happened to be in that part of Glendale and I said to myself, this would be a good time to pay Burlew that long over due visit. It was Sunday morning and I found him home. The first thing he did was to take me to the back of the house. Pointing to a large native sycamore tree, he said, "How do you like that?" My gaze followed the tree to it's top, about seventy feet I guessed. "Gee," I said, "That's a beauty." "Well," he said, "I bought that from Theodore Payne in a gallon can." Then turning and pointing to a large Big-Leaf Maple, he said, "I bought that too from you in a gallon can."

"My," I said, "It makes me feel very old, how long ago is it?"

"It's just fourteen years," he replied. Then he showed me some Live Oak trees he had raised from acorns. We measured these and they averaged fourteen inches in diameter. I could hardly believe it.

Later, I told this story one day at the Rancho Santa Ana Botanic Garden to Mrs. Bryant and Frederick Law Olmsted, the landscape architect. Mr. Olmsted said, "Your story reminds me of an occurrence that happened on an estate where we were doing some work back east." There were a number of fine trees on this place, I don't remember what kinds Mr. Olmsted said they were but that doesn't matter. One day some tree experts came around and looked at these trees, one specimen in particular interested them. They measured it and then took a photograph of it. The owner of the estate came out and they introduced themselves to him and said, "We hope you don't mind us photographing this tree. It is the finest specimen we have been able to find around here. You know, Mr. So-and-so, this tree is 150 years old." The owner listened to them very intently and when they had finished he said, "Well, gentlemen, that is very interesting, because I planted it."

Theodore Payne at right, in front of his seed store at 345 South Main, Los Angeles, c. 1906

Interior of 345 South Main

Payne's nursery at 440 South Broadway, Los Angeles, 1903

Early magazine ad for Payne's wild flower seed mixes

Theodore Payne about 1903

Two tall palms, Washingtonia robusta, *on a vacant lot at Hill & 4th Streets, Los Angeles, ready to be moved*

Digging up the palms to be moved. Payne at center in white hat

*Moving the palms by horse trailer to Abbot Kinney's new development in
Venice, Ca. along Washington Boulevard, c. 1905*

Theodore Payne at train station in Indio, Ca., c. 1912

Payne at left, digging well at a ranch in Thermal, Ca.,
co-owned with Modjeska Ranch foreman John Ruopp,
c. 1913

Theodore Payne collecting wild seeds

Theodore Payne (second from left) and men gathering eucalyptus seeds, early 1920s (photo by T. P. Lukens)

Mrs. Alice Payne at gate of Payne residence in Atwater Village, Los Angeles, c. 1926

BRIEF HISTORY OF A LIFE IN HORTICULTURE

Harvest Brodiæa - *Brodiæa grandiflora.*

A Life in Horticulture

I was born at Manor Farm, Church Brampton, Northamptonshire, England, June 19, 1872, being the fifth of a family of six boys. My father died when I was less than three years old, so I do not remember much about him, but he and my mother had planned and planted a very beautiful garden. As a child I was passionately fond of flowers; I always found the first primroses to bloom in the spring. I knew all the haunts of the wild flowers in the neighborhood. My mother was fond of flowers and had studied botany; she taught me the names of the plants. I used to collect seeds of the different flowers in the garden and put them in packets for friends. I had my own little garden in which I worked and took a great deal of pride. So it became generally understood while I was still quite young, that when I grew up I would be a horticulturist.

My early education was at home. We had one small room set aside as the school room, and a governess came in every day to teach us. The first one was Miss Tarry who came from a neighboring village. She did not have much success with me, I did not want to learn, I would much rather work in my garden or play out in the farm yard. She almost gave me up as hopeless. Then she left and Miss Warren took her place. We got along well, and I began to make some progress.

My mother died when I was eleven years old and when I was twelve I was sent to Ackworth School in Yorkshire. It was a Quaker boarding school and the same school where my older brothers and also my father had gone before me.

At Ackworth I joined a natural history society. While being interested in natural history generally, botany was my special choice and I was elected secretary of the botanical section. My collection of pressed wild flowers was awarded the first prize. It was here at Ackworth that I had my first lesson in conservation. A rare plant which had been known in only one locality had become almost extinct. Our natural history society obtained some roots from another source and we planted them in the place where they were becoming extinct.

There was a limited number of gardens for boys who were interested in horticulture. You could obtain the rights to one of these gardens by buying it from some other boy who was willing to relinquish his claim or who was leaving school at the end of the term. Mine was handed down to me by my brother. I took a great interest in this garden and had a fine display of flowers especially perennials.

After leaving Ackworth, I was apprenticed for three years to the firm of John Cheal & Sons, Lowfield Nurseries, Crawley, Sussex, to learn the nursery and seed business. The guardians of my father's estate paid a premium of fifty pounds (about $250.00) to this firm for teaching me the business. My indenture of apprenticeship was drawn up legally, signed by all parties before witnesses, and bore government stamps for the amount of fifty shillings. The firm paid me five shillings (about $1.25) a week for the first two years and six shillings a week for the last year. I went through all the different departments of this business, viz. greenhouse department, growing plants under glass, propagating under glass, grafting rhododendrons, clematis, etc., budding roses in the field both bush and tree types, budding and grafting fruit trees, pruning and training fruit trees, espalier, cordon, bush and standard, propagating ornamental trees and shrubs, layering, etc., propagating perennial and rock garden plants.

One fall I spent over six weeks making cuttings of conifers and other evergreens.

The firm had a very complete seed department, housed in a building especially built for this purpose. They handled a very complete assortment of flower and vegetable seeds catering to a high class private estate trade. They also had a good business in farm seeds. I spent one season in this department.

We worked from seven in the morning to six at night. In the winter and spring we went back every evening except Saturday and worked a few hours in the office, making out invoices, writing letters, posting books, etc.

In the season we had to attend flower shows. For a large show like the Crystal Palace in London, there were generally three of us in charge of the exhibit. In smaller, one day shows, one would have to handle it alone. The exhibit would be prepared the day before, then early next morning one of the men would drive me to the depot. I would see the cases loaded safely on the train, then at the destination get them hauled to the place where the show was to be held, stage the exhibit and stay there all day talking to the visitors or taking orders for dahlias, roses, chrysanthemums, fruit trees, or whatever it might be that was on exhibition.

After the show was over, the cases had to be hauled to the train and brought back; generally it was late, and I would leave them at the depot to be hauled the next day. I, of course, had to walk home a distance of nearly three miles, so it was frequently 11:30 or 12:00 o'clock when I reached home.

Fortunately, there was not generally more than one of these shows in a week, but one time there happened to be three, all in different places. I had no sooner reached home and had a few hours sleep, then I had to start out again.

All this early training became valuable to me in later years. There are a number of trained nurserymen in California and some trained seedsmen. But I do not know of anyone else who had a complete training in both lines.

I spent much of my leisure time roaming the woods and fields, studying the wild flowers. I collected seeds of some kinds and grew them in my garden. The firm I was with specialized in landscaping and one of their clients wanted a large area laid out as a wild garden. I was entrusted with the work of collecting all the wild plants for this project. On completion of my apprenticeship I continued with the same firm for about eighteen months, holding a position in the seed department.

In the spring of 1893, I decided to come to California and on June 3rd, sailed for New York. After spending four or five days in New York, and a week in Chicago visiting the World's Fair, I came on to Los Angeles, arriving here on June 28th. I worked a few days at picking apricots at $1.50 per day. Then I secured a position as gardener to Madame Helena Modjeska, the famous Polish actress, at her country estate "Forest of Arden," Santiago Canyon, Orange County. I held this position for two and one half years, and it was here in the Santa Ana Mountains that I first began to take an interest in the wild flowers of California.

In April 1896, I entered the employ of the Germain Fruit Company, Seed and Plant Department, (now Germain Seed Company) in charge of the flower, tree and palm seed department. While holding this position I prepared all the catalogues for the firm and handled much of the correspondence, especially where any technical information was required.

In the summer of 1897 I took a trip home to England for a few months and while there crossed over to the continent.

In those days Germain's handled pampas plumes which were then grown extensively here in Southern California. I represented the firm on this trip and sold over 40,000 of these dried plumes in London, Hamburg and Erfurt. I became manager of the firm in 1902.

In the spring of 1903 I resigned this position, having decided to go into business for myself. But first I took a trip back home to England. On the way I called on the leading seed stores in Chicago, Philadelphia, New York and Boston. While in England I visited the large seed firms in London. Then I took a trip over to the continent, calling on many of the leading horticulture establishments in Belgium, Holland, Germany and France. On this trip I booked orders for several hundred dollars worth of seeds which I knew were not obtainable in California. I made some business connections which continued more or less until the time of the second world war.

Returning to Los Angeles about the first of October, I began looking for a location for a seed store, and on November 3rd, bought out the nursery of Hugh Evans at 440 S. Broadway. This was formerly the Lyon and Cobbe Nursery founded in 1890. To this business I added a complete seed department. In 1905 I moved to 345 S. Main Street, maintaining a nursery sales yard in the rear of this and adjoining stores. A few years later I bought a nursery at 33rd and Hoover Streets, which I used for growing grounds.

I handled a complete line of vegetable seeds, flower seeds and some farm seeds. Of tree, shrub and palm seeds, I had the most compete stock of any firm in the country. I published a 64 page general catalog each season and a bulb catalog in the fall.

At least once a year I made a visit to all the local nurseries, going as far as Redlands, Riverside and Santa Barbara. On these trips I took orders for tree and shrub seeds. I also kept posted on what each nurseryman had in the way of nursery stock. My store on Main Street became a sort of clearing house for the nurserymen. I bought and sold many thousands of dollars worth of stock. Customers would come to me for stock wanted and I usually knew where to get it. One season I shipped five carloads of citrus trees into Ventura County, another year five carloads into the Sacramento Valley. In 1913 I sent three carloads of ornamental stock to San Diego for use in landscaping the grounds for the 1915 Exhibition.

I made a special study of the Eucalyptus, and collected seed of most of the species grown in California. I soon became headquarters for these seeds in the United States, and when the Eucalyptus boom came along, about 1907, I received some very large contracts for seed. In 1911, 1912 and 1913 I made large shipments of this seed to Brazil. In 1912 I shipped 125 lbs. of cleaned seed of Blue Gum (*Eucalyptus globulus*) to Germany. The order, of course, was for re-shipment to some other country. Two years later I shipped 100 lbs. of the same kind to France. I also had a large mail order trade in Eucalyptus seed in California, Arizona, Texas, Florida, Isle of Pines, Mexico and South America. One season I collected about 1500 lbs. of Eucalyptus seeds of different species, but mostly *E. tereticornis* and *E. rostrata*.

When I first came to California, what impressed me perhaps more than anything else was the wonderful native flora. But as the years went by it was with deep regret that I saw the wild flowers so rapidly disappearing from the landscape. I made up my mind that I would try to do something to awaken a greater interest in the native flora. Thus it was that I began to specialize in the growing of wild flowers and native plants. I collected seed of a few kinds of wild flowers, grew them and offered the seed for sale.

Little or no success attended this first venture, it being generally conceded that it was foolish to waste time on "wild flowers." As a demonstration I secured the use of a vacant lot in Hollywood and sowed it with wild flower seeds. I went to Walter Raymond of the Raymond Hotel in Pasadena and asked him for the use of a piece of ground for sowing wild flower seeds. Mr. Raymond readily consented and the following spring there was a splendid display. I also secured the use of two lots in Pasadena, one on Green Street and the other at the corner of Lake and Colorado, which I sowed with wild flower seeds. All these plots were greatly admired and I received complimentary letters from many people. This was really the beginning of wild flower planting.

My first wild flower catalog was a very modest little booklet published about 1906.

While roaming around in the San Fernando Valley, I noticed that certain areas would produce a succession of flowers and color effects—yellow predominating at one time, blue at another, and so on. I wondered if the same effects could be produced artificially so I began to experiment by mixing several kinds of seeds, sowing them and watching the results. It was in this way that I perfected my wild flower mixtures which have since become so popular.

In 1915 I laid out and planted a five acre "Wild Garden" at Exposition Park, Los Angeles, using native flowers and plants exclusively. This garden contained five main groups of trees, viz., a sycamore grove, an oak grove, a redwood grove, a big tree grove, and a pine grove, together with smaller plantings of native shrubs, perennial plants, bulbous plants, and a large area of annual wild flowers. In all the garden contained 262 species, the whole being a reproduction of a natural landscape, with one specimen of each kind adjacent to a walk, labeled with both the botanical and common names. It was greatly admired by many thousands of people from all parts of the country and received generous press notices in all parts of the world. It was used as an educational feature by the schools and did much to awaken interest in native flowers and trees.

I wrote many articles on wild flowers and native plants and lectured in nearly all the towns of Southern California, taking for my title, "Preserving the Wild Flowers and Native Landscapes of California." Referring to one of these lectures the late Mrs. E. J. Bissell made the following statement. "It was your lecture to the Garden Club of Santa Barbara at Mrs. Campbell's house on Middle Road in Montecito that gave us the idea and inspiration to start the Blaksley Botanic Garden. Furthermore, had it not been for your establishment this garden could not have come into being, because there was no where else to obtain the necessary material in seeds and plants." It is a fact that over eighty percent of the native trees, shrubs and wild flower seeds used in this garden in its earlier stages of development were produced in my nursery.

In 1919 I was retained by Mrs. Lora J. Moore, (later Mrs. Knight), to take charge of the landscaping of her new estate on Toro Canyon Road, Montecito, Santa Barbara. This property consisted of about 140 acres, a considerable portion of which was heavily wooded with live oak trees. There was also a beautiful canyon running through the property and several open grassy meadows. I laid out several trails in different directions and established colonies of wild flowers and bulbs.

I planted a very complete family orchard of about two acres and also a large vegetable and cut flower garden, with a glass house and lath house for propagating purposes.

One fourth of the water in Romero Canyon went with the property and the reservoir stored 1,200,000 gallons of water, much more water than was needed, so the surplus was allowed to run down the canyon, making a live stream almost the whole year round. This made it possible to do some very interesting development in this canyon. A trail starting near a bridge just inside the property followed the canyon, crossing and re-crossing the stream more than thirty times, and terminating only a short distance from the residence.

I laid out quite a large informal rose garden and fitted it into the natural landscape by surrounding it with quite a heavy planting of native shrubs.

The house was built in 1922 of Mission type architecture in a square, surrounding a patio, with a large live oak tree in the center. The residence looked out onto a green meadow of about 1500 feet in length, gradually rising to a small hill with the mountains in the background. On top of this hill I planted 121 Monterey Pines naturally grouped. The meadow I sowed with perennial rye grass which survived the summers without any artificial watering. I also sowed 30 pounds of *Sisyrinchium bellum* "Blue Eyed Grass" in this meadow. The effect when in bloom was very pleasing, and as these plants are perennial, they bloomed year after year.

The estate was closed during the summer so was especially adapted to native planting with it's rest period during the dry season. There was so much natural beauty on the place that the work consisted mostly in assisting nature by adding a touch here and there. The place abounded in beautiful native rock which was used in building retaining walls, steps, etc. The gardener's cottage at the entrance was built entirely of this rock, also the lower portion of the main residence.

The development and maintenance of this estate lasted for eight years. I kept ten men on the place, a separate bank account in a Santa Barbara bank, and made two trips each month to Santa Barbara. In 1927 I turned the place over to my foreman, George P. Hendry, who had been with me from the beginning.

As a result of this project I secured other landscape work in Montecito, including the Jackson estate adjoining Mrs. Knight's, the Hammond place (5 years), Jones estate and others in Santa Barbara and Ojai valley. These different projects continued up until 1939.

In 1919 I entered into a partnership with Ralph D. Cornell in the landscape profession. We opened up an office in the I. W. Hellman Building under the name of Ralph D. Cornell and Theodore Payne, Landscape Architects. This was entirely separate from any other business and was for the purpose of handling larger landscape projects. As Ralph had Pomona College on a yearly basis and I had Mrs. Moore's place, we were assured of our expenses before we started in. This partnership lasted for five years, during which time we handled some very interesting developments, including the Mason estate in Pasadena, Torrey Pines Park, Occidental College, C. C. Teague residence in Santa Paula, other residences, parks and subdivisions. We were also retained for several years in an advisory capacity to the Park Department of the City of Pasadena.

Our venture was financially successful from the beginning and was a very enjoyable experience for both of us. However, in 1924 Ralph had an exceptionally attractive offer of a partnership in another firm without the investment of any capital, so by mutual agreement we decided to dissolve our partnership.

In 1922 I purchased 10 acres of land fronting on Los Feliz Boulevard and moved my nursery to this location. I had a very complete nursery, handling a large assortment of exotic plants, but specializing in native plants and wild flower seeds. About 6 acres was devoted to the nursery and buildings and the remainder to the growing of wild flower seeds and bulbs. I maintained my office and headquarters at 345 South Main Street until the summer of 1931, when I moved this and the seed department to the Los Feliz address. I developed quite a good landscape business in the local field which has continued more or less up to the present time.

In 1926 I was requested by Mrs. Susanna Bixby Bryant to accompany her on a visit to the Rancho Santa Ana to select a site for the botanic garden. The Rancho Santa Ana Botanic Garden was founded in the following year and I served on the advisory council for over 20 years, up until the time the garden was moved to Claremont. I also served for many years as horticultural consultant, making two trips each month to the garden, supervising the propagation of plants in the nursery and planting of the different areas of the garden.

In 1941, through four very unjust assessments for street improvements, storm drains, etc., amounting to over $27,000.00, I lost most of my property. After this, having less than one acre of ground left, I decided to confine my efforts to native plants and wild flowers exclusively. Thus what was started as a hobby now became my sole business.

Starting my career in horticulture in 1888, I have now spent 70 years of my life in this field. Of this period 65 years have been in California and 55 years in business for myself.

During this period I have introduced into cultivation in California between 400 and 500 species of wild flowers and native plants and made them available for general use. Some of these plants were introduced into Europe a long time ago but were unknown in California gardens. A few of the most important of these introductions are: *Fremontia mexicana*-1919; *Ceanothus cyaneus*-1922; *Berberis nevinii*-1920; *Lupinus paynei*-1919; *Cupressus forbesii*-1935, *Platanus racemosa*-1910; *Alnus rhombifolia*-1913; *Rhus laurina*-1910; *Rhus ovata*-1910; *Rhus integrifolia*-1910; *Eriogonum giganteum*-1924.

Other introductions, but not California natives, are Arizona Cypress-1908; *Dimorphotheca aurantiaca*-1912; *Tithonia speciosa*-1918; Pike Sapote-1926; *Aquilegia longissima* (out of horticulture for a long time) re-introduced in 1929.

Besides the Eucalyptus already mentioned, I shipped quantities of other seeds to many parts of the world, including England, Germany, France, Sweden, Island of Cyprus, Africa, Mexico, several South American countries, New Zealand, Tasmania, Australia and some other countries. Some of the largest orders were, 400 pounds *Washingtonia filifera*, "California Fan Palm", 600 pounds *Atriplex semibaccata*, "Australian Saltbush", for the Argentine Republic, 500 pounds *Pinus ponderosa*, "Yellow Pine", for the government of Australia. Several shipments of 100 pound lots of *Cupressus arizonica* went to France.

Several young men have received their early training in horticulture in my establishment. Among these was Dr. Carl B. Wolf, who afterwards went to Stanford University, and upon receiving his degree was engaged as botanist for the Rancho Santa Ana Botanic Garden, a position he held for fifteen years. Four have become successful landscape architects in California and Washington. One is with the Federal Government in charge of a soil conservation nursery. Others hold responsible positions in public and private institutions and one or two have nurseries of their own.

On my eightieth birthday, June 19, 1952, I was honored by the Southern California Horticultural Institute and presented with a bronze plaque in recognition of my work in conserving the native flora of California.

In the fall of 1954 I received the Pacific Coast Nurseryman award of a silver cup for outstanding achievement in horticulture.

ORGANIZATIONS TO WHICH I NOW BELONG
or in which I was active in former years

Life member, Fellow, Past President, Southern California Academy of Sciences. Joined the Academy in 1898, became a director in 1919 and served for over thirty years on this board. Now on the Advisory Board of the Academy. Honorary Life Member, Southern California Horticultural Institute. Life Member, The Wilderness Society, Washington, D. C. Life Member, National Audubon Society, New York. Life Member, Save the Redwoods League. Fellow, Royal Horticultural Society of England. Life Member, Nature Conservancy, Washington, D. C. Member, California Arboretum Foundation., Inc. Member, Los Angeles Audubon Society, Calif. Audubon Society. Honorary Member, Hollywood Horticultural Society. Member, California Botanical Society; Southern California Botanists; the Museum Association of Los Angeles County Museum. Various Conservation groups. Charter member of the Nature Club of Southern California. (This membership continued for over twenty years until the organization disbanded.) Charter member of the California Association of Nurserymen. (Continued this membership for more than twenty years and wrote twelve or more annual reports on native vegetation.)

President, Los Angeles County Horticultural Association for two years. This organization met once a month in Los Angeles and was active for several years up until the time of the first World War. President, Wild Flower Club of the Southwest Museum. Supervised the most complete wild flower show yet held in California with 53 Species on exhibition. The club disbanded when the policy of the museum was changed excluding the natural sciences. President, Southern California Arboricultural Association, one term. This organization was active for several years, holding a two day convention each year. These were held in Riverside, Redlands, Santa Ana, Pasadena, Los Angeles, and some other cities. This organization had a marked influence on tree planting in many of the communities of Southern California. Operations were suspended during the first World War and were not resumed.

In the summer of 1929 I was appointed as a collaborator with the Department of Agriculture, State of California. This was during the Mediterranean Fruit Fly scare and my duties were to examine and report on native plants with fleshy fruits which might be hosts for the fruit fly.

Also see: *Who's Who in California*, Vol. 1, 1942-1943; *Sunset Magazine*, April 1918; *National Geographic Magazine*, April 1942; Home Magazine, *Los Angeles Times*, Dec. 1, 1943; *Christian Science Monitor*, Dec. 14, 1946; *Nature Magazine*, May 1947; *American Home*, February 1948; *Lusca Leaves*, Autumn 1954; *Golden Gardens*, October, 1955; *Who's Who in California*, Second Edition-1957; and Home Magazine, *Los Angeles Times*, March 23, 1958.

THEODORE PAYNE CHRONOLOGY

1872   June 19: born in Northamptonshire, England.

Active during school years in botanical society; made collection of pressed plants. Apprenticed to a nursery firm at age 16 for thorough training in nursery and seed business.

1891   Saw large display of California native plants at The Royal Botanical Gardens at Kew in England.

1893   Came to California at age 21 and had charge of the gardens on Madame Modjeska's ranch in Santiago Canyon, Orange County (2 1/2 years). Began his interest in California wild flowers.

1896   Employed by Germain Seed (then Fruit) Company.

1903   Established his first nursery and seed business at 440 S. Broadway, Los Angeles. Began collecting wild flower seeds as a hobby.

1905   Moved business to 345 S. Main where office remained until 1931.

Began specializing in California wild flowers, native plants and eucalyptus. Purchased growing grounds at 33rd St. and Hoover.

Planted vacant lots in Hollywood and Pasadena with native wild flowers.

Created wild flower garden for Raymond Hotel in Pasadena.

1906   Published first catalog: *California Native Flower Seeds*.

1907   Married Alice Noyes in San Francisco.

1913	Became President of Wildflower Club of Southwest Museum and laid out its native garden. Developed herbarium there.

1913   Became President of Wildflower Club of Southwest Museum and laid out its native garden. Developed herbarium there.

Co-owned ranch in Thermal with John Ruopp, foreman at Modjeska Ranch.

1915   Developed first public area in Los Angeles planted entirely with natives: a 5-acre wild garden at Exposition Park (now site of the rose garden), containing 262 species of California native trees, shrubs and wild flowers.

1919   Formed 5-year partnership with Ralph D. Cornell. Designed large landscape projects: Pomona College, Occidental College, Torrey Pines Park. Designed Washington Park for City of Pasadena.

1922   Moved nursery to 10 acres at 1969-99 Los Feliz Blvd. on land he purchased.

1926   Provided ideas and plant materials for Blakesley (now Santa Barbara) Botanic Garden.

1927   Assisted Mrs. Susanna Bixby Bryant with siting and design of original Rancho Santa Ana Botanic Garden in Orange County. Helped to relocate the Garden to Claremont in 1951.

Maintained private estate landscaping commissions throughout Southern California: Beverly Hills, Bel Air, Pasadena, and Santa Barbara.

1939   Created native plant garden with 176 species at California Institute of Technology, Pasadena (later site of Norman Church Laboratory).

Continued publishing articles and speaking about loss of wild flowers.

1952	June 19: 80th birthday. Honored by Southern California Horticultural Institute and given honorary life membership.
1958	Developed a 5-acre native plant garden at Descanso Gardens, La Canada.
1960	Los Angeles County Board of Supervisors set aside 320 acres in Antelope Valley, near Llano, to become Theodore Payne Wildlife Sanctuary, dedicated January 28, 1961. Theodore Payne Foundation incorporated to carry on his work.
1961	After 58 years in business, turned over stock of seeds, plants and equipment to The Theodore Payne Foundation for Wild Flowers and Native Plants, Inc., (TPF) a non-profit organization to perpetuate California's native flora.
1962	June 19: 90th birthday. Celebration at Administration Hall of Los Angeles County Supervisors.
1963	"Man of the Year" Award by California Garden Clubs, Inc. May 6: died in Los Angeles. Papers and library donated to TPF. Introduced into cultivation over 430 species of wild flowers and native plants during his lifetime.
1966	Current 20-acre site of Theodore Payne Foundation in Sun Valley, California, donated by Eddie Merrill.
1969	Acquisition of adjacent 2-acre property for Foundation office.
1983	Beginning of TPF Spring Wildflower Hotline
2004	First Annual TPF Los Angeles County Native Plant Garden Tour

Payne's 10-acre nursery and sales yard at 1969-99 Los Feliz Boulevard, Los Angeles, mid 1920s. Gladding McBean (Franciscan Pottery) factory is at right

Visit the Nursery and Display Grounds

INTENDING planters are urged to visit the nursery and display grounds at 2969-2999 Los Feliz Boulevard, where they may select at leisure and with care the plants or trees best suited to their requirements. Courteous, well informed nurserymen will help to solve the many problems that confront the average planting scheme; the what, when, and how to plant, and where; the deciduous and evergreen; the color, form and foliage best suited to shady places, to sunny places, on hillsides or in dry locations; the ultimate growth of selected varieties, and dozens of other important considerations that must be correctly determined if the final effect is to be satisfactory.

Here, too, will be found an assortment of exotic and native trees, plants and shrubs, roses, annual and perennial flowering plants, bedding and border plants, ferns and palms, wherein a most exacting or most trivial desire may be gratified—easily and pleasurably.

Drive out when the planting urge is upon you, or in when driving by.

How to Reach the Nursery and Display Grounds
BY AUTOMOBILE

From Downtown Section. Through Second Street Tunnel out Glendale Boulevard to Riverside Drive, which is just before crossing the river bridge. Turn left to Los Feliz Boulevard and right to nursery.

Western and Southwestern Sections. North on Vermont or Western Avenues to Los Feliz Boulevard, turn to right and follow through lower portion of Griffith Park to the nursery on the left hand side of the boulevard.

Eastern and Southeastern Sections. Drive crosstown to Vermont or Western Avenues and follow as above, or through Second Street Tunnel out Glendale Boulevard to Riverside Drive, which is just before crossing the river bridge. Turn left to Los Feliz Boulevard and right to nursery.

Northern and Northeastern Sections. Drive out San Fernando Road to Los Feliz Boulevard, which is three blocks beyond the Pacific Electric tracks in Glendale. Turn left. Nursery is on the right hand side, one long block beyond the Southern Pacific tracks.

Pasadena and San Gabriel Valley. West on Colorado Boulevard to Brand Boulevard in Glendale. South on Brand Boulevard to Los Feliz Boulevard and west to the nursery, one long block beyond the Southern Pacific tracks on the right hand side.

San Fernando Valley Section. Drive south on San Fernando Road to Los Feliz Boulevard. Turn right. Nursery is one long block beyond the Southern Pacific tracks, on the right hand side. Via Ventura Boulevard, drive south over Cahuenga Pass to Hollywood Boulevard, turn left to Western or Vermont Avenue, again left to Los Feliz Boulevard and right to the nursery.

BY STREET CAR OR BUS

Take Glendale car from new Subway Station on Hill Street, between Fourth and Fifth Streets. Get off at Atwater Station, cross tracks and walk north on Boyce Avenue to the nursery. Pasadena-Hollywood-Ocean Park bus stops at the entrance.

THEODORE PAYNE

Downtown at
345 South Main Street
VAndike 6481

2969-2999 Los Feliz Boulevard
Telephone OLympia 3609
Los Angeles

Back cover of Payne's 22nd annual catalogue, 1926

Front of new nursery building on Los Feliz Boulevard, c. 1925

Building after landscaping growth, 1927

Mrs. Payne in lath house at nursery headquarters, 1927

Picnic at Bluebird Ranch, Glendora, 1929, Theodore Payne in center, Ralph Cornell at left, unidentified colleague at right

Early ad for the landscaping partnership of Ralph Cornell and Theodore Payne

Theodore and Alice Payne with unidentified child, in the Sequoias, late 1920s

*Payne among tree lupines, a species he discovered,
named in his honor by Dr. Anstruther Davidson,
noted Los Angeles botanist*

Mrs. Payne enjoying the tree lupines

Payne's 80th birthday celebration, Los Angeles City Hall, June 19, 1952. From left: Dr. William Hertrich (superintendent of Huntington Botanical Gardens), Hugh Evans, Marvin Braude, Mr. & Mrs. Payne, Roy Wilcox, Paul J. Howard. Payne's 90th birthday was celebrated at the offices of the Los Angeles County Supervisors in 1962

Theodore Payne at his nursery, c. 1952

Dedication of Theodore Payne Wildlife Sanctuary, Antelope Valley near Llano, Ca., with Cub Scouts, January 1961

"Theodore Payne Himself," at dedication of his 5-acre native garden, Descanso Gardens, La Canada, Ca., 1959. Alice Payne's name tag on that occasion stated simply "His Wife."

Payne's Legacy Today

Tree-Poppy - *Dendromecon rigidum.*

The Modjeska Ranch Revisited

by Ellen K. Lee

Helena Modjeska Foundation

Theodore Payne's memoir, *Life on the Modjeska Ranch in the Gay Nineties*, remains the best account of daily life on the Orange County ranch owned from 1888 until 1906 by the Polish actress, Helena Modjeska, and her husband, Karol Bozenta Chlapowski. Modjeska named her ranch Arden, for Shakespeare's Forest of Arden, the setting of his pastoral play, *As You Like It*.

After Modjeska's death in 1909, most of the ranch land along the banks of Santiago Creek was subdivided. By the time Payne published his illustrated memoir in 1962, the remaining 14-acre home site was privately owned and seldom seen by outsiders.

Today "Arden: The Helena Modjeska Historic House and Gardens" is a United States National Historic Landmark, owned by the County of Orange, maintained by its Department of Harbors, Beaches and Parks, and open to the public for regularly scheduled tours.

Theodore Payne's legacy lives on. His memoir is a valued guidebook for park rangers and docents. Garden volunteers turned to his list of twenty of Modjeska's favorite roses when they planted a memorial rose garden with many of the heritage varieties that he recalled as Modjeska's favorites. Double pink oleanders and Turk's Cap, both mentioned in his memoir, still bloom beneath palm trees that he planted more than a century ago. Visitors and school children learn about the gardener's shack, Payne's first California home, where he first became aware of the beauty and value of the wild flowers and native plants that he found on the hills and in nearby canyons.

A two-mile stretch along Santiago Creek, once the Modjeska Ranch, is now named Modjeska Canyon. More than three hundred houses are hidden among ancient olive trees pruned long ago by Theodore Payne, and beneath the oaks and sycamores where a stage Rosalind walked in her own Forest of Arden.

The Theodore Payne Foundation and Nursery

by Frances Schneider Liau

When Theodore Payne came to California in 1893, he saw mountainsides exploding with wild flowers, marveling at their profusion and diversity. They became his life's work. He valued their inclusion in urban settings and offered them for use. As he witnessed native habitat shrinking under pressure of development, he focused his attention on preservation.

In 1960, to ensure that his actions, his vision and his voice would carry on, Payne's colleagues established the foundation that bears his name as a non-profit membership organization. Its mission, even more relevant today, is to promote, preserve and restore California native landscapes and habitats; to collect and make available native plants and seeds; and to educate the public about California flora and natural history.

On 22 acres in Sun Valley, Los Angeles, the Foundation operates a nursery, seed center and bookstore. Visitors to this natural setting, seeking replacements for exotic plants or reprieve from the lawnmower and sprinkler, walk Wild Flower Hill and browse in the display areas. Over 600 species and selections of native plants are offered for sale, including seed mixtures created by Payne himself. Staff advises about plant choices for successful growth. Small classes assist gardeners with designs for eye-catching results.

Payne believed that by becoming familiar with the plants of a region we are taught by them to feel truly at home. The Sun Valley site is a resource for information about the beauty and benefits of incorporating natives into Southern California's landscapes to reestablish habitat. Foundation programs include a website, library and archives, the Spring Wild Flower Hotline, seasonal sales events and a native plant garden tour.

Theodore Payne taught by example, as a mentor to young people who became leaders in natural science and landscape architecture. Continuing this tradition of education, the Foundation hopes to inspire learners of all ages by engaging their active participation and interest. The sycamore-shaded nursery that carries on his work welcomes volunteers and visitors to share this legacy.

INDEX OF PLANTS, PLACES, AND PEOPLE

Abyssinian Banana, 40
Acacia greggii, 170
Ackworth School, Yorkshire, England, 187-88
Agripina Rose, 169
Alnus rhombifolia, 198
Amole, 19
Andreas Canyon, 170-72
Antelope Valley, 215
Apple trees, 135-36
Aquilegia longissima, 198
Arden, 75, 85; Historic House and Gardens, 219
Arizona Cypress, 198
Atriplex semibaccata, 167, 198
Australian Saltbush, 167, 198
Baldwin, Lucky, 169
Beach Wallflower, 131
Beloperone californica, 171
Berberis nevinii, 198
Berlin, Germany, 108
Big Leaf Maple, 173
Bishop Pine, 163
Blaksley Botanic Garden (later Santa Barbara Botanic Garden), 162, 194
Blue Dawnflower, 39
Blue Eyed Grass, 195
Blue Gum, 140, 155, 173
Booth, Edwin, 69, 73, 75
Bozenta, Count Karol (Chlapowski), 15, 58, 61, 67, 68, 79
Brea Canyon, 90-92
Brodiaea grandiflora, 185
Bryant, Susanna Bixby, 174, 197

Bush Lupine, 155
Bush Penstemon, 38
Bush Sunflower, 115, 131
California Fan Palm, 40, 198
California holly, 115
Canary Island Date Palm, 39
Cannas, 39
Capistrano, 49-50
Carob, 138
Carpinteria, "Big Grape Vine," 93
Cat's Claw, 170
Ceanothus arboreus, 163
Ceanothus cyaneus, 197
Chamise, 115
Chase, J. Smeaton, 170
Chatsworth tunnel, 121-22
Chicago World's Fair, 14
Chuparosa, 171
Church Brampton, Northamptonshire, England, 160, 187
Claremont, Ca., 197
Cocos plumosa, 117
Cocos romanzoffiana, 117
Colorado Desert, 104, 158
Comarostaphylis diversifolia, 163
Cooper, Ellwood, ranch, 95
Cornell, Ralph D., 170, 171; partnership with Payne, 196, 208, 209
Corona, Ca., 127
Coulter Pine, 101
Cracow, Poland, 65-68
Crystal Palace, London, 189
Cupressus arizonica, 198
Cupressus forbesii, 198

Cypress (city in Orange County), 143-45
"Dante's Inferno," 31
Davidson, Dr. Anstruther, 104-107, 150, 167, 211
Dendromecon rigidum, 217
Descanso Gardens, La Canada, Ca., 216
Desert Apricot, 170
Desert Sand Verbena, 158
Dimorphotheca aurantiaca, 198
Doheny, E. L., 118
Dracaena draco, 94
Dragon Blood, 94
Durbin, Maud (later Mrs. Otis Skinner), 57-62
Echinocystis fabacea, 87
Einstein, Albert, 172
El Toro, 15, 47
Eriogonum arborescens, 163
Eriogonum giganteum, 198
Eucalyptus, at Ellwood Cooper ranch, 95, 140; in Libya, 153; gathering seed, 183
Eucalyptus diversicolor, 140
Eucalyptus globulus, 173, 192
Eucalyptus pilularis, 140
Eucalyptus rostrata, 132, 143, 192
Eucalyptus tereticornis, 140, 143, 192
Evans, Hugh, 165, 191, 213
Exposition Park, Los Angeles, 193
Fern Trees, 125
Fithian Ranch, Santa Barbara, 93
Flores' Peak, 41
Forest of Arden, Modjeska's home, 75, 190

Franceschi, Dr. F., 153
Frederick the Great, King of Prussia, 108, 111
Frederick William I, King of Prussia, 108, 111
Fremontia mexicana, 197
Gazania splendens, 39
Germain Seed Company, 63, 112, 190
Gillette, Mrs. King C., 171
Goat Nut, 170
Grevillea robusta, 125
Harding Canyon, 32, 43, 63
Harleston, Northamptonshire, England, 160
Harvest Brodiaea, 185
Hazardia cana, 163
Hedge Mustard, 167
Hertrich, Dr. William, 213
Hoffman, Ralph, 162, 163
Hollywood, 125
Horehound, 45-46
Huntington Botanical Gardens, 213
Idylwild, in San Jacinto Mountains, 101
Indio, Ca., 181
Ipomoea leari, 39
Ironwood Tree, 163
Island Buckwheat, 163
Island Oak, 163
Jacaranda, 40
Japanese Wineberry, 39
Johannesburg, South Africa, source of ostrich eggs,112
John Cheal & Sons, Lowfield Nurseries, Crawley, Sussex, England, 188-90
Jojoba, 170
Joshua Tree, 94
Kinney, Abbot, 123, 180
Knight Estate, Montecito, 194-96

Lamb's Tongue, 39
Larkspur, 38
Laurel Canyon, 96
Lea, General Homer, 128-30
Lemonade berry, 115
Leucadendron argenteum,
    93-94
Libya (Tripoli), 153
Ligustrum nepalense, 167
Live Oak Trees, 174
Lukens, T. P., 183
Lupinus paynei, 150, 198,
    211
Lyonothamnus floribundus
    asplenifolius, 163
Maidenhair fern, 39
Malibu Ranch, 116
Malvastrum rotundifolium,
    105
Malvaviscus mollis, 39
Mariposa Lily, 38
Mary Semple Aster, 169
Matilija Poppy, 11, 38
Meadow Rue, 38
Mexican Fan Palm, 123
Modjeska Canyon, 220
Modjeska, Helena, 15, 18-21,
    52, 58-59, 63; early life in
    Poland, 65-66; theatrical
    career in America and
    Europe, 67-75
Mohavea viscida, 105
Monterey Pines, 195
Mountain mahogany, 115
Mount San Jacinto, 101
Nature Club of Southern
    California, 162
Navarro de Andrade,
    Edmundo, 139-42
Occidental College, 196
Oleanders, 39
Olives, 29
Olmsted, Frederick Law, 174
Ombu Tree, 137

Ontario, Ca., 125-27
Orange, town of, 13
Ostrich Farm, South
    Pasadena, 113
Paderewski, Ignace, 17
Palm Canyon, 158
Pampas grass, grown by acre,
    95
Pasadena, Raymond Avenue
    opera house, 52
Payne, Alice (Mrs. Theodore),
    131, 133, 183, 210, 212,
    213, 216
Penstemon antirrhinoides, 38
Penstemon heterophyllus
    australis, 38
Phytolaca dioica, 137
Pike Sapote, 198
Pinus muricata, 163
Pinus ponderosa, 198
Platanus racemosa, 198
Prunus fremontii, 170
Quedlinburg, Germany, 109-
    111
Quercus tomentella, 163
Rancho Santa Ana Botanic
    Garden, 174, 197, 198
Raymond, Walter (and
    Raymond Hotel,
    Pasadena), 193
Red Gum, 132
Redondo Beach, 131
Rhus integrifolia, 198
Rhus laurina, 198
Rhus ovata, 198
Romneya coulteri, 11, 38
Roses, old fashioned at
    Modjeska Ranch, 19-20,
    39, 85
Ruopp, John, 15, 60, 181
San Antonio Heights (above
    Upland, Ca.), 125-27
Sand verbena, 115
San Fernando Valley, 193

Santa Ana, 54, 89-92
Santa Barbara, 93, 118, 153
Santa Barbara Natural History Museum, 162
Santa Cruz Island, 162-64
Santa Monica, 114, 116, 165
Santa Susanna, 150
Santiago Canyon, 13, 19, 42, 83
Sao Paulo, Brazil, 139
Seven Oaks, San Bernardino Mountains, 97-100, 128-29
Sexton, Joseph Nursery, 95
Shepherd, Theodosia B., Nursery in Santa Barbara, 63, 93
Silverado Canyon, 46-47
Simmondsia californica, 170
Sisymbrium officinale, 167
Sisyrinchium bellum, 195
Skinner, Cornelia Otis, 57
Skinner, Otis, 59, 75
Small Leaved Privet, 167
Sonoratown, Los Angeles, 34
South African Silver Tree, 93-94
Spadra, 91
Spotted Mallow, 105
Stachys lanatum, 39
St. Vibiana's Cathedral, Los Angeles, 64
Summer Holly, 163
Sun Cups, 115
Sun Valley, Ca., 221
Sycamores, 165, 173
Theodore Payne Foundation and Nursery, Sun Valley, Ca., 221

Theodore Payne Wildlife Sanctuary, Antelope Valley, Ca., 215
Thermal, Ca., 104, 106, 158, 181
Tithonia speciosa, 198
Tomato 'Payne's Victory', 154
Tree Poppy, 217
Turk's Cap, 39
Tustin, fog thick as London, 54
University of California Forestry Station, Santa Monica Canyon, 139
"Unter den Linden," Berlin, Germany, 108
Venice, California, 123, 168, 180
Ventura County, citrus dilemma, 146-49
Violet Beard Tongue, 38
Warsaw, Poland, 67-68
Washingtonia filifera, 40, 170, 198
Washingtonia robusta, 123, 179, 180
Watsonia, 21
White Snapdragon, 131
White, Stanford, 16, 81
Wild buckwheat, 115
Wild cucumber, 87
Wild heliotrope, 115
Yellow Pine, 198
Yoch, Florence, 21
Yucca arborescens, 94